LIVING THE
TRUTH

ALSO BY KEITH ABLOW, MD

Nonfiction
How to Cope with Depression
Medical School: Getting In, Staying In, Staying Human
Anatomy of a Psychiatric Illness
To Wrestle With Demons
Without Mercy
Inside the Mind of Scott Peterson

Fiction
Denial
Projection
Compulsion
Psychopath
Murder Suicide
The Architect

LIVING THE
TRUTH

TRANSFORM YOUR LIFE THROUGH
THE POWER OF INSIGHT AND HONESTY

KEITH ABLOW, MD

LITTLE, BROWN AND COMPANY

New York Boston London

Little, Brown and Company
Hachette Book Group USA
237 Park Avenue, New York, NY 10169
Visit our Web site at www.HachetteBookGroupUSA.com

First Edition: May 2007

Names and some characteristics of individuals portrayed in this book have been changed so that the confidentiality of each is completely protected.

The excerpts from *Blood and Grits* by Harry Crews on pages 64–65 and 188, copyright © 1979 by Harry Crews, are reprinted here by permission of John Hawkins and Associates, Inc. The excerpt from "The Gift Outright" on page 24 is from *The Poetry of Robert Frost,* edited by Edward Connery Lathem. Copyright © 1934, 1969 by Henry Holt and Company. Copyright © 1962 by Robert Frost. Reprinted by permission of Henry Holt and Company, LLC.

Library of Congress Cataloging-in-Publication Data

Ablow, Keith R.
   Living the truth : transform your life through the power of insight and honesty / Keith Ablow. — 1st ed.
       p. cm.
     ISBN 978-0-316-01781-7
   1. Self-deception.   2. Honesty.   3. Insight.   4. Self-esteem.   I. Title.
BF637.D42A33   2007
158.1—dc22   2007001953

10 9 8 7 6 5 4 3 2 1

Q-FF

Printed in the United States of America

For my children, Devin Blake and Cole Abraham

CONTENTS

Contents

LIVING THE
TRUTH

Introduction

During my fourth year of medical school at Johns Hopkins, one of my mentors was Stuart Fine, MD, a charismatic and warm man who had risen through the ranks of academia to become a professor of ophthalmology at the prestigious Wilmer Eye Institute. Dr. Fine was one of the world's most prominent experts in the macula, the tiny area of the retina that boasts the highest concentration of receptors for light. Macular degeneration is the leading cause of blindness in the United States.

I was helping Dr. Fine research the extent to which laser treatment halts the progression of macular degeneration, in the hope that my work would win me one of the coveted residencies in ophthalmology at either Wilmer or the Massachusetts Eye and Ear Infirmary.

Then one day Dr. Fine called me into his office and changed my life. "Please take a seat," he said, nodding at one of the armchairs emblazoned with the Hopkins insignia that sat in front of his desk.

The desk itself commanded my attention, its surface completely covered with giant plastic models of the eye, a collection of eye-shaped crystal and marble paperweights, dozens of ophthalmology journals, reams of research data.

"I want to talk to you man-to-man," he said.

I stopped looking at his desk and looked at him.

He took off his round tortoiseshell glasses.

My stomach sank. I worried that I had fallen short of expectations and had not only squandered my chance to train at Wilmer but also disappointed a man I greatly admired, a father figure who had had me to his home for dinner, boasted of my intellectual prowess to his wife and daughter, and given me the sense that I might be heir to his professional legacy.

"I think I can help you get one of the residency positions you want," he said.

A wave of relief washed over me. "Fantastic," I said.

He smiled indulgently. "It would be fantastic," he said, "if you really wanted one."

"Of course I—" I started to protest.

He held up a hand. "Just hear me out," he said. He stared so intently at me that I wondered if he could see clear through to my retinas. "When I was your age, all I was reading in my spare time were books and journals about the eye. It fascinated me."

I smiled and nodded, trying to match his enthusiasm.

He shook his head. "I've seen what you read when you aren't working. You read books about psychiatry, and you read novels. And I've seen you with patients. You ask them all kinds of questions about who they are. And you really listen to them. You can't help looking into their lives." He smiled. "I can't help looking into their eyes."

Dr. Fine was drawing a distinction between his truth and mine, and I didn't like it. I felt as if I were being accused of something.

"I can see the whole world in the macula," he went on. "And

I'm not sure you can. I think you're a psychiatrist, not an ophthalmologist. But if you tell me I'm wrong, I'll do everything I can to make you the best ophthalmologist you can be. It's your decision."

I stayed up that entire night, thinking. A big part of me wanted it to be morning already so I could rush to Dr. Fine's office, all smiles, and tell him that I wanted to be an ophthalmologist. That way he could make good on his promise to help me become one. I had worked hard to get the chance. My parents would be proud of me. They would call their friends. My classmates would be envious.

When I went to Dr. Fine's office the next morning, though, I was a changed person. I couldn't play the role of his heir apparent anymore. His words had been so clearly stated, the *truth* embodied in them so powerful, that they had brought me too close to my own reality. And it initially made me feel lonely and lost.

"Well?" he asked.

"I think you're right," I said. I took a deep breath, let it out. "I think what really moves me is the way people think, not the way they see." And then I said something much more revealing. "I wish that wasn't the case, but it is."

Dr. Fine took off his glasses again. "Why do you wish that?" he asked. "It's who you are."

That question took me most of my four years of psychiatry residency at New England Medical Center, including psychotherapy with Dr. James Mann, one of Boston's premier analysts, to answer. Because in my wish for something other than an authentic life were nestled a number of other very painful (and, ultimately, very empowering) truths.

Chief among the realities that I had wished to avoid was the fact that I had never been convinced my father loved me. He'd said he did, loudly and many times over the years, but I didn't *feel* it deep down, where it matters.

My plans to become a surgeon genuinely pleased him. It

made no difference if I became a heart surgeon, a plastic surgeon, a neurosurgeon, or an eye surgeon. My academic success was one of the only things—maybe *the* only thing—I was certain he liked about me. He'd proudly told his friends about my grades in high school and college. He glowed when my acceptance letter to medical school arrived. And in those moments, I could—and did—convince myself that all was well between us.

Becoming an ophthalmologist was one way I had unconsciously planned to perpetuate that fiction. He had made it clear to me that he didn't think much of psychiatrists.

Dr. Fine telling me that he didn't buy my life story not only started me on a truer career path but also started me on a path of self-discovery that has never ended. To this day, the more painful it is to think about an aspect of my life, the more sure I am that those thoughts hold promise for my continual rebirth as a real and powerful individual.

Everything I have done of value in my professional life has been about burrowing relentlessly toward the truth. It is more than my career, more than my passion. It is my personal mission. This includes my work as an investigative journalist; my work as a forensic psychiatrist, getting to the bottom of the real workings of the minds of violent men and women; my work as a novelist, creating characters who are true to their souls (or who pay a terrible price for not being so); my work as a columnist, revealing sometimes disturbing and sometimes moving realities about the human condition; my work as a television talk show host, encouraging people to confront their pain and share it with others; and most important my work as a psychiatrist, delving past the surface layers of my patients' personae to unite them with their inner truths, making them whole again and capable of miraculous personal growth.

After listening to so many stories, I have developed a sixth sense for when my patients are withholding the truth from me, from themselves, or from both of us. I have palpable confidence that they will be able to make the journey into their pain and back out—and be better for it.

The next step in my professional life is this book. It is my most ambitious attempt to help people do what I finally did— face the truth about the past, however uncomfortable, sad, or frightening—and experience the remarkable power that comes from that journey.

My aim in the chapters that follow is to deliver many of the benefits of long-term psychotherapy. These benefits include a clear vision of how important relationships, critical life events, and God-given strengths and weaknesses conspire to influence one's self-concept, hopes, and fears. From this new vantage point, a person can clearly see a gap between *what is* in his or her life and *what could be* in his or her life once negative influences are confronted and overcome. With the courage that comes from unmasking that genuine potential, groundbreaking changes in friendship, romance, and career are all suddenly within reach.

Part of the art of psychotherapy is creating the proper emotional environment to reassure a person that it is essential *and* safe to dig for that treasure. That's partly what the rest of this book is about. I will share with you the rationale for living the truth while introducing you to good and decent and courageous people who have done just that and, as a result, have revitalized their romances, friendships, marriages, parent-child relationships, even their careers. I've chosen to tell you about these particular people because their struggles for autonomy, self-esteem, willingness to trust, and ability to love are bound to reflect parts of your own struggles, thereby bringing your truth closer to the surface.

I am eternally grateful to these people. Through the miracle of empathy, you will find that their journeys of self-discovery have already quietly set the stage for your own journey. Their stories are true, but I have had to make changes in this book to protect my patients' identities. I have taken a bit of dramatic license here and there in reconstructing our dialogues and have changed the particulars of their situations so that they are unrecognizable.

Your journey here will be a working partnership with me. I'm going to ask you to do some "soul-searching" as you read this book, just as I ask my patients to do when they come to my office. I've included exercises and will ask you to write down some thoughts and answer some questions. You may want to write your responses in the spaces provided here or to keep them in a separate notebook. Some of what you write will be very private; you may be writing about loved ones with whom you don't want to—or are not ready to—share your innermost thoughts. It might be a good idea to find a special place to keep this book or your notebook if you don't want your writings read by others.

When I told my father that I had decided to become a psychiatrist, he said, "To me, it's not like being a real doctor."

He was right. Being a psychiatrist means working at the interface of medicine and spirituality, with a willingness to believe both in science and truths that are immeasurable but no less compelling. It means keeping your eyes open and helping other people do the same, even in utter darkness, wherever the truth might lead.

This book has that journey as its goal. I ask you to take the journey with me.

Our Partnership

People find me when they need to. They need to improve their marriages, build better relationships with their kids, or fall in love with someone worthy. They need to be more courageous in pursuing their dreams, to leave addictions behind, or to rid themselves of anxiety or depression. They know it's time to change, but they aren't sure how to make that change.

That's why you found me, too. You bought this book because something in your life is *not* what it should be.

Chances are that before buying this book you tried many ways of avoiding the real problem. The human mind has a bad habit of denying what needs fixing, deep down. Whether becoming involved in whirlwind romances with the wrong men or women, drinking too much alcohol, moving from city to city or job to job, using drugs, becoming mired in obsessive thinking, or compulsively overeating, people often spend decades running away from the truth before they finally feel enough pain or get tired enough or just plain fed up enough to turn and face it.

MY PROMISE

Your sadness, anxiety, boredom, or anger is your wake-up call. It feels bad right now, but it's a gift. Because until your heart and soul cry out for a fuller life, you can't begin the journey in earnest.

With this book in hand, you can. We can now be partners in dramatically improving your life. I feel the same commitment to you as I would if you had walked into my office as a patient. You've shown up, which took courage. And I promise my best effort to honor that courage by helping you find out what is limiting you, and giving you powerful tools to overcome it.

In turn, I need you to promise me—and more important *yourself*—that you won't lose faith as we work together. I intend to help you uncover the roots of your psychological limitations so you can rid yourself of them once and for all, and grow confidently in whatever direction you choose. If I succeed, there will be times when thinking about what you've read will actually make you temporarily more sad, more anxious, or more angry. But you can't let that stop you.

The pledge that follows is a symbol of your willingness to stay with me, even when it hurts. Please take it seriously. You should sign it only if you are committed to making real change by facing the truth about your life. And only then will our journey truly have begun.

YOUR PLEDGE

I know the journey of living the truth holds the promise of making me a more honest, loving, and powerful person, but that getting there will hurt. I agree, therefore, to try faithfully to overcome the resistance to this book that is likely to arise within me. I acknowledge that the resistance could take many forms— misplacing the book (in which case I will replace it), deciding to "skim" it or read it while distracted by television (in which case I will reread it more carefully), deciding I feel too sad to keep reading it or that half of it has done enough for me (in which case I will turn the page and forge ahead). I pledge to finish it, cover to cover, and to do so within the next thirty days.

Jonathan Silverman

Signed

3-31-09

Dated

PART ONE
OPENING
YOUR EYES

The Pain-to-Power Principl

The origins of self-deception run deep inside us. As we mature, small lies we tell ourselves about the past build into an impenetrable web of denial and fantasy that conceals our pain. This web has to be unraveled if we are ever to find our way back to the people we were meant to be.

We all tell ourselves lies; we all have buried truths. Most of us fear revealing them, even to ourselves. So we leave them buried and do whatever it takes to keep them there, sometimes forever. Our lives become more and more inauthentic. We forget the Pain-to-Power Principle—that coming to grips with the truth, rooted in the past, is our greatest source of power.

One of the ways we can learn to live the truth is by example. When we hear of someone who has shown the courage to look honestly at the most difficult chapters of his or her life story—whether he or she suffered through divorcing parents, abuse, loss of a dear friend, a spouse's infidelity, an illness, or growing up with an alcoholic—we can be inspired to do the same.

Empathy is a big part of that inspiration. Listening to some-

ne talk about the toughest parts of his or her life triggers an in-
ernal barometer of truth in us, a part of the soul that resonates
only with genuineness. And when that barometer tells us we are
in the presence of truth being revealed, it also tells us that the
person speaking the truth is more, not less, powerful as a result.
We feel this way because we respect and admire that person. We
connect with the humanity of that individual. And in a way that
can actually transform our lives, we connect a little bit more with
our own humanity, our own hidden truths.

We get courage by observing and listening to stories of courage. That's a kind of miracle.

I've seen it again and again while hosting my show. One person after another has sat with me in the studio and found the resolve to stop running from his or her past, to start facing pain
buried for many years, to finally feel that pain and move beyond
it. It not only empowers each and every one of them but also empowers many of those watching in our live studio audience.
Thousands of attendees and viewers have told me—in person or
by letter, e-mail, or phone—that they have lived through some of
the same trials and tribulations as my guests, and that the bravery of those guests in breaking through decades of denial provided a big part of their motivation to face their own truths.

The same inspiration can come from reading life stories,
and that's why I will share with you the experiences of several of
my patients. Our journeys toward living the truth have the power
to transform not just our own lives but the lives of everyone
around us.

LIVING IN DENIAL

Four months before she came to see me, Nicole, forty-six, would
have said her life was very nearly perfect. She had been married
nineteen years and had a healthy daughter, seventeen, and son,
fourteen. She worked part-time as the office coordinator for her

husband, Grant, a successful Realtor. She was in close touch with her sister, forty, and both her parents. She had friends, a dog, two cats, and a Volvo SUV.

Sure, she sometimes wondered whether drinking a glass of wine or two to get to sleep could be a problem, but plenty of people didn't sleep well and plenty of people enjoyed their wine. And yes, there was also the way she went on shopping sprees to lift her mood when she felt down for more than a day or two, but a few extra dresses or pairs of shoes didn't seem like the end of the world. Even the fact that she didn't have much interest in sex anymore didn't seem so weird. After all, she'd lived and worked with the same man for nearly two decades—not exactly the ultimate recipe for passion.

Then, shortly after her daughter, Kelley, was accepted to a nationally recognized design school, Nicole's mood really started slipping. She was thrilled to see Kelley pursuing her dream, so she couldn't understand why she wasn't on cloud nine with her. She figured maybe with all the excitement and worry of the application process, she had simply given way to fatigue. Maybe visiting schools had been more exhausting than she knew. She remembered feeling the same way after her wedding, when the ceremony and celebration and honeymoon were over.

This time, however, turned out to be different. Her mood continued to slip. Within three months, despite Kelley's growing excitement about going to college, Nicole found herself tearful at times. She felt exhausted and couldn't concentrate at work. She began arguing more with her husband, especially when he bothered her about her drinking. She was up to three glasses of wine at bedtime, usually around nine o'clock, earlier when she could think of an excuse. She had no sexual desire whatsoever. In dark moments after midnight, she even doubted whether life was worth living.

She began to wonder if her real problem might be her marriage. She certainly didn't feel anything close to romantic love anymore. When she thought about it, she probably hadn't for many years. But she didn't *want* to think about it.

By avoiding the pain in her life, Nicole was no different from most of us. In working with thousands of patients over the last fifteen years, I have found that human beings have a reflex reaction to psychological pain no different from their reaction to physical pain. We withdraw from it. We try to avoid thinking about not only the painful aspects of our lives today but those in the past, all the way back to childhood.

This should come as no surprise. No one wants to feel bad, and the human instinct to seek pleasure and avoid pain (including painful recollections) has been a central principle in philosophy and psychology since the time of the ancient Greeks. Sigmund Freud called it the "pleasure principle."

Indeed, we accept the notion that the mind uses many "defense mechanisms" to distance us from bitter realities—we repress our emotions, we rationalize our behaviors, we distort past events. Chief among these mechanisms is denial, in which we unconsciously ignore distressing facts about ourselves or others. Denial can make us "look the other way" in the face of evidence that our spouses are unfaithful or our children have turned to drugs. It can make us immune to feedback from friends and loved ones who warn us about our addictions or other self-defeating behaviors.

Nicole might never have come to see me, in fact, were it not for her fourteen-year-old son, Nathan. Nate was a high school football player and all-around jock, not one to talk about his feelings, so when he got choked up and told Nicole he felt as if he had "lost his mother," she decided it was high time she tried to "find herself." She heard me interviewed on a local radio station, called my office, and booked an appointment.

The first time we met, I could see that Nicole wasn't just well put together—she was perfectly put together. Everything was in its place—her designer clothes, her jewelry, her makeup, her hair. She was physically fit and looked younger than forty-six. But she also looked worried. She avoided eye contact. And more than once, she clenched and unclenched her fists, as though to wring the tension from her hands.

I nodded at them. "You're having a hard time," I said.

She looked down at her hands and let out a long breath. "I never thought I'd be saying this," she told me, "but I think I may need something."

"You mean, a medicine?"

"My sister's on Zoloft. She says it helps her."

I knew why Nicole was asking for Zoloft right off the bat: part of her was still searching for some way to cover up the trouble in her life instead of getting to the bottom of it. Sitting with a doctor whom she knew had made it his life's work to help people get to the truth, she was making a last-ditch effort to avoid that very process.

"Zoloft might be part of the answer," I told her, "but I'd have to understand much more about *you* and your life to know."

She clenched her fists again.

I leaned toward her. "Tell me what's wrong," I said.

That was enough to make her eyes fill up. "Nothing," she said. She twisted her engagement ring back and forth. "My marriage. The way I am around my kids . . . losing my temper. I'm a complete mess."

"You're a person," I said. "That's always messy."

She looked directly at me for the first time.

"What's happening in your marriage?" I asked.

She smiled even as a tear escaped her eye. She wiped it away. "Not a lot—which is kind of the problem. We're . . . existing." She shook her head as though trying to stop herself from saying more. The impulse to keep one's truth—especially one's pain—secret is among the most common, powerful, and toxic elements of human nature. "Grant is a wonderful person," she said.

"He's been a great provider for almost twenty years. He's never hurt me."

If all my years as a practicing psychiatrist have taught me one thing, it's this: listen for what people *do not* say. All Nicole could come up with at the moment about Grant was that he made money and wasn't abusive. That left out a lot of other desirable qualities.

I knew Nicole needed permission to tell me what she was really feeling. And since she had already hinted at her reality, I gave her an opening. "He's wonderful, but . . ."

A new look came into her eyes, a kind of sudden, unblinking focus I had seen take hold in other patients once they became convinced I really wanted to hear their truths and would not judge them. "But I'm bored to tears," she said flatly.

"And have been for how long?"

"Honestly?"

I waited.

"Probably since I've known him."

Nicole had come in asking for a prescription, maybe thinking that she had slid into a depression over the course of a few months, and we were already journeying back twenty-three years, to when she first met Grant. "What did you think of him when you met him?" I asked.

"That he was a real gentleman," she said. "That he would make a good husband and father—even if he was pretty, well, predictable." She squinted as if looking back all those years—which, in fact, she was. "I'd been through a really bad breakup just before I met him," she said. "I wanted someone stable."

"Who had you broken up with?" I asked.

"Oh, God." She laughed and actually blushed—*more than twenty years later.* So much for those who would deny the power of the past. "He was a complete mess."

A complete mess. Those were the same words Nicole had used to describe herself just moments before. And that was no coincidence. Listening carefully to Nicole had led me to my questions, which had led directly to the unconscious connection she now felt with her lover from decades before. "What kind of mess?" I asked.

"The worst kind," she said. Her expression brightened, and she suddenly looked ten years younger. "A troubled artist. Your typical bad boy."

"'Bad,' meaning . . . ?"

"You know. Wine, women. Not to mention the fact that he was broke."

"You weren't about to go there," I said.

She chuckled, shook her head. "I'd already been there."

"How so?"

"With my dad."

Nicole had come in for what she thought would be a quick fix—Zoloft—and come face-to-face with unresolved feelings about her father. We had traveled thirty or more years in about thirty minutes.

"Your dad?" I asked.

"Ancient history," she said. She looked away again.

"Doesn't sound like it," I said. "Here we are, talking about him."

"What can I say? He was a lot more interested in his scotch, the track, and other women than he was in my mother, my sister, or me."

It was worse than that one-liner might indicate, though, and Nicole told me the rest during a few more sessions. Her father would disappear for days at a time. Other women would call the house, setting the stage for screaming matches and occasionally even physical fights between her parents. Sometimes her dad gambled away everything he made as a laborer, leaving the family without food.

Once I knew that "ancient history," I knew why it seemed so important to Nicole to look perfect. She felt anything but perfect inside. Part of her was still the little girl whose father might be sober one night, drunk the next, smiling and generous when he came home from the track a winner, violent when he had lost everything. No wonder Nicole would have traded passion with a troubled artist for the predictability and stability Grant offered. She couldn't risk that her artist-lover would turn out to be no different from her dad. And that's one reason she would have felt somber after exchanging marriage vows—those vows were motivated partly by fear. They were partly about living life and partly about avoiding it.

"It doesn't help anything," Nicole said, "that I work with Grant and live with him. We're together 24-7."

"Why did it turn out that way?" I asked.

She shrugged. "He needed the help, and I didn't have much of a plan," she said. "I mean, I had fantasies about interior design or whatever, but I had no training or anything." She laughed. "I figured I'd at least know where he was all the time."

"Unlike your father," I said.

She stopped laughing. "I suppose," she replied.

"Did you ever pursue your love of design?"

"Just stuff in our house," she said. "I'll leave the rest to Kelley."

My skin turned to gooseflesh, as it does whenever the past becomes palpable in the present. It was clear to me now why Kelley leaving for design school had triggered Nicole's depression. Kelley was living out dreams that Nicole had once had for herself, dreams she had buried in order to create the safe family life she craved. Now, with her daughter off to design school, where she might even fall head over heels for an artistic, romantic, unpredictable man, Nicole was feeling the loss of what she had given up in exchange for stability—pieces of herself.

Why did it take Nicole almost losing herself entirely—thinking she might not want to live—before she gathered the courage to begin to find herself again? Because she thought she could avoid her pain. She had decided—partly consciously, partly unconsciously—to use alcohol, material possessions, great attention to her physical appearance, and even her commitment to her marriage vows to avoid thinking about *why* she had opted out of passion and *why* she had traded her own professional goals for the chance to keep an eye on her husband.

The reason was obvious to me, but I wanted to make it obvious to Nicole. I wanted to bring her face-to-face with the truth she had run from her whole life. Only that kind of reckoning with the early chapters in her life story could leave her free to imagine, and then live, wonderful chapters in the future. "So what do you think your dad loved more," I asked her, "the gambling, girls, and booze . . . or you?"

She sat in silence for several seconds. Her eyes filled with tears again. "Not me," she said finally. "I guess I never really wanted to admit that. I mean, I was the one by his bedside every day for six months after he was diagnosed with cancer. I think I just wanted to hear him say . . ." She stopped herself.

". . . that he loved you," I said.

Tears ran down her cheeks.

"Had he ever told you that?" I asked.

She swallowed hard. "No," she said. "And he never did." She looked down as though ashamed.

I let a few moments pass. "You know the worst part?" I asked Nicole.

She looked at me.

"Part of you still thinks he was right—that you're not lovable. That's what any little girl would think, growing up with a father who was incapable of caring about her. And that's the same part of you, by the way, that tells you that you have to keep tabs on your husband to keep him honest, instead of challenging *him* to grow if he wants to keep *you* around. It's the same part of you that won't express your passion for design. There's always that little voice in the back of your head saying maybe you're not worthy of love—not even your own."

"So how do I get that voice to stop?" she asked.

I smiled. "By listening to absolutely everything it has to say."

THE JOURNEY FROM PAIN TO POWER

Why would I prescribe such a painful journey? What could Nicole gain by looking back at such an unhappy time in her life? The answer is simply this: her *self,* the brilliant potential for self-esteem and self-expression she was born with. That treasure was buried under chapters of her life story she had been frightened to look at, chapters that quietly taught her to settle for being less than she could really be.

Only by hearing out the little girl inside her—the one saying that she was never worthy of her father's devotion—could Nicole, now an adult and a mother, nurture herself as she might a child, by finally focusing on the truth that she was born to a man who never made her *feel* worthy. And only by truly grieving that misfortune could she stop blaming herself for it.

Almost all of us live at some distance from the painful truths about our lives, sometimes going to great lengths to continue avoiding them. To the extent that we do, we actually diminish ourselves.

To find the self-esteem we need to live full lives, we have to look back to when and how we were deprived of it.

In truth, our pain is the source of our power. That's the Pain-to-Power Principle.

Robert Frost put it this way:

> *Something we were withholding made us weak*
> *Until we found out that it was ourselves*

MASKING THE PAIN

About two years ago, a forty-year-old highly successful CEO named Richard came to see me. A year before, he had begun experiencing symptoms exactly like those of a heart attack. All of a sudden, he would feel nauseated and light-headed. His chest would tighten, his pulse would race, and his skin would get clammy. Convinced he was dying, he would call 911 and be rushed from his apartment or his office to the emergency room. But each time, his EKG and lab studies would prove he hadn't suffered a heart attack at all.

When a stress test and angiogram both came back normal, Richard's cardiologist correctly diagnosed him with panic disorder—the symptoms of which can be indistinguishable from cardiac disease—and wrote him a prescription for Paxil.

Everything was fine for about three months. Then Richard's symptoms returned. His cardiologist increased his Paxil and added some Klonopin, a tranquilizing medicine. That bought him another nine months. Then, at the leading edge of winter, his mood slipped dramatically, he lost all motivation, and he began to feel like a "complete fraud." Everything he had achieved had been, he said, a fluke. He had no real intelligence and no genuine leadership ability.

Richard's cardiologist increased his Paxil yet again—but this time to no avail. Richard's mood continued to plummet. When he broke down in tears at a business meeting, his cardiologist referred him to me.

The first time I saw Richard, he looked like a deflated superhero. His longish blond hair, which I could imagine elegantly styled, was a mess. His suit needed pressing. His green eyes were bloodshot, with dark circles beneath them. The way he leaned forward, shoulders hunched, made it seem as if he literally needed help standing up. He displayed what psychiatrists call "flat affect," showing very little emotion of any kind—no smiling, no tears.

I added a second antidepressant to Richard's regimen in order to help him cope with his symptoms, but I told him from the beginning that those symptoms were being fueled by earlier chapters in his life story that he had been loath to "read." Without his opening them and learning what had set the stage for his suffering, no medicine would be powerful enough to keep his anxiety and depression at bay forever.

Everything on the spectrum—from worry to panic, from unwieldy moods to bipolar disorder, from a few glasses of wine to take the edge off to full-blown alcoholism—turns out to be much more like an abscess than a headache. The pain is always a symptom of something deeper that needs healing.

If you took Advil or Tylenol or Percocet for a walled-off abscess, you'd get relief for weeks, or even longer. But eventually the painkillers would stop working, the pain would worsen, and other symptoms would arise, including fever. That's because the underlying pathological process—the infection—would be quietly invading more and more healthy tissue.

The only way to truly heal such an abscess (painful as it might be) is to move directly into it, open it, and let it drain.

It is no different with the painful emotional conflicts inside us.

Toward the beginning of our first meeting together, I asked Richard essentially to take the Living the Truth Pledge, to assure me that he would do everything in his power to continue exploring his story rather than run away from it. He agreed.

It wasn't until nearly the end of the hour that he mentioned that when his symptoms began two years before, he had just broken up with a woman.

"I really thought she was the one," he said. "But she threatened to throw me out, and I don't respond to that kind of thing."

Again, I noticed that Richard showed no emotion. He didn't

seem sad and he didn't seem angry. "How long had you been living together?" I asked.

He shook his head. "Oh, we weren't living together. I just meant she threatened to dump me."

Odd turns of phrase often have real meaning.

Richard seemed to be saying that his girlfriend's threat to break up with him felt like being "thrown out" of his home. I kept that in the back of my mind.

He sighed. "She told me I had to either marry her or take off. She was thirty-five. That whole biological-clock thing."

"How long had you been dating?"

"A little over six years."

"You weren't ready to get married?"

"I thought I was a few times," he said. "I even bought a ring once. But I couldn't go through with it."

Richard hadn't said he didn't *want* to get engaged. He'd said he *couldn't*. "Why not?" I asked.

"Who knows? Maybe I can't love anyone, or maybe I'm unlovable. I don't know anything anymore."

That gave me hope. Not knowing was a good place to start. "Let's figure it out," I said. "Is there anyone you can say with certainty *does* love you?"

"My parents. That's it," Richard said immediately. "God knows where I'd be without them." He was silent a few moments, then sighed again and checked his watch. "I think we're running over."

Running, maybe. "I'm okay for time, if you are," I said.

"Sure," he said tentatively.

"So tell me how you knew your parents loved you."

"I was an only child. They did everything for me," he said. "Best prep school in the country, best college. They always believed in me. Right after I graduated college, my dad actually let me run the London office of his consulting company. Eighteen employees."

"Which prep school did you go to?" I asked.

"Phillips Academy, in Massachusetts."

"Quite a school," I said. "Did you grow up nearby?"

"No, Syracuse," Richard said. "There really isn't anything like Phillips anywhere near there."

That disclaimer—that Richard's parents had had no choice but to send him hundreds of miles away for his education, beginning in the ninth grade—brought me to my next question. "How did you feel, going away to school?"

"Overwhelmed. It was the best."

"Overwhelmed" was another curious choice of words. "You didn't miss home?" I asked as offhandedly as I could.

"I was homesick, sure," he said. "But everybody adjusts, right?"

Everybody wasn't in my office. Just Richard. "What was the adjustment like for *you?*" I asked.

The way Richard described feeling "homesick" sounded a lot like depression. He couldn't concentrate on his work, lost interest in the sports he loved, had trouble sleeping, dropped ten pounds, and suffered from vague physical symptoms such as transient headaches and stomachaches. It went on for months. "Sounds really tough," I said. "Did you have to go back home for a while?" I asked.

He shook his head. "Not an option."

"Why's that?"

"My dad had to bail out a company in Paris for four months—until right after Christmas. My mom went over there with him. They left right after I did."

Being homesick is one thing. Being without a home is another. As I talked with Richard during our next few meetings, the latter seemed closer to the truth. Starting in ninth grade, his parents had sent him away to very prestigious schools, but they had never really welcomed him back. Even when he finished college and planned to move back to Syracuse to work in the "home office" of his father's consulting company, his dad had another plan: he sent him off to run the London office instead. His mother didn't object.

I thought of the way Richard had described his girlfriend's ultimatum that they either get engaged or end their relationship after six years. *She threatened to throw me out.* "Were you upset about being sent to London?" I asked him.

He shrugged. "How could I be? Talk about a kid in a candy store. There I was at twenty-two, running a company."

That didn't sound like pure fun. It sounded anxiety provoking, too. "You were alone," I said, "thousands of miles from home."

"I was a pretty clingy kid when I was little. It's better they made a clean break of it. I probably never would have."

I felt I had a pretty clear sense of why Richard's relationship with his girlfriend had ended the way it had. Unable to believe she truly loved him (because he had never truly felt loved by anyone, *including* his parents), he had been too frightened to give her the commitment *she* needed to feel secure, the love *she* needed to feel at home. And when she had threatened to leave, he had taken that as proof that he had been right to doubt her devotion.

Trouble was, he didn't really buy that logic himself. Somewhere deep inside, Richard knew he was just using his girlfriend as a stand-in. He was blaming her for abandoning him rather than admitting that it was his parents who had (and in lots of ways, it turned out, even before ninth grade).

When you lose the woman you love over a case of mistaken identity, it's more than enough to give you panic disorder.

My skin turned to gooseflesh again. The past was making itself known in the present. "Why would your parents ever want a 'clean break' from you?" I asked Richard.

"I didn't mean it that way," he said.

I kept looking at him.

He looked away.

I reminded him of the pledge he had taken to search for his truth, even if it hurt.

He sat in silence for twenty or thirty seconds, a very long time without words. Then his lip began to quiver, and his eyes filled up. It was the first gut-level emotion he had shown in my office. He was rejecting the fictional life story he had settled for decades earlier. "They had each other," he said. "I'm really not sure I ever had either one of them."

It didn't take more than a few additional meetings for Richard to realize that he hadn't been able to get engaged because he hadn't trusted his girlfriend to stay with him, to create a true *home* with him.

"So what are you going to do now?" I asked him.

"It's not like she'd ever take me back," he said.

"How do you know that?" I asked.

"I just do."

"You think you do," I said, "because your parents never took you back. That doesn't mean it's true this time."

He called his former girlfriend that very day, an act that required tremendous courage. To do it, he had to accept that his parents (not his girlfriend) had failed to give him a sense of security, that they hadn't made him feel genuinely cared for. He had to admit that loving them without being convinced they loved him back had left him wary of putting his heart on the line ever again. Then he had to do just that.

When you are willing to hurt in order to heal, people respond to your bravery and honesty. Your pain becomes your power. Richard's girlfriend not only took his call but also listened to what he had to say and took him back. She said she would give him the time he needed to trust her. And in doing so, she gave him the very thing his parents had failed to: the certain knowledge that he could go home again.

LIVING A MEDICATED LIFE

Richard's cardiologist was right to understand that Richard was not suffering from heart disease. He was suffering from failure to *know* his heart. His panic attacks made him think that his body was giving out—when, in truth, his soul was giving up on living a "fraudulent" life.

Richard's cardiologist was also right to prescribe Paxil to treat his symptoms, and he was right to send him to me to get to the bottom of his panic disorder. All too often, however, patients (and their doctors) are much too willing to settle for drugs instead of exploring the roots of their problems.

Many of my patients come to me thinking all they need is a prescription. No wonder—there are pills for everything now, and many psychiatrists and plenty of family physicians are all too happy to write out scripts within fifteen minutes of patients' reporting symptoms of anxiety, panic, or depression, or that they suffer from weight problems, addictions, insomnia, or attention deficit disorder.

Now, more than ever before, we're discouraged from doing the right thing: digging deep into our life stories to learn what we can from every chapter.

Psychiatric medicines such as Lexapro (for depression), Adderall (for attention deficit disorder), and Ambien (for insomnia) are miraculous tools for relieving the unbearable sadness, unwieldy inattentiveness, and crippling lack of sleep that can make self-reflection impossible. But their discovery has given birth to the dangerous myth that they are a complete solution not only to these conditions but also to anxiety, unhappiness, and angst. Many family physicians, nurse practitioners, obstetricians, pediatricians, and psychiatrists treat millions of Americans with these medicines not just to facilitate but to replace coming to grips with painful truths about their lives and using those truths to become more complete, compassionate, and confident people.

It doesn't work. People often come to me for treatment having "listened to Prozac" instead of to their pain and having taken medicine instead of taking themselves in hand. They have been living on borrowed time emotionally, feeling better about themselves without knowing themselves any better. And when they come face-to-face with family strife or grief or financial problems or depression or panic attacks, they are one or two or five years deeper into denial, making the journey back to truth that much more difficult (though never impossible).

Think of the millions of children treated exclusively with Ritalin for attention problems who have very real and painful issues in their lives that they would rather *not pay attention to.* If the medicine helps them focus on schoolwork while ignoring troubling emotional issues for five or ten years, they will build self-concepts based on those unresolved issues, with low self-esteem as the result.

Imagine, for example, a ten-year-old girl who quietly suspects, or unconsciously senses, that her father is having an affair. Or a four-year-old boy whose mother has a miscarriage in her seventh month that is barely discussed with him. Or a nine-year-old girl who tries not to notice her fifteen-year-old brother peeking at her while she's getting dressed. Or a painfully shy twelve-year-old girl who is shunned by boys. Any one of these children might become distractible to the point that he or she is diagnosed with attention deficit disorder. And Ritalin might well allow them to focus on schoolwork and feel happier. But the three girls are likely to incorporate anxiety and fearfulness into the emotional patterns with which they respond to men in the future. And the boy may well experience unwieldy anxiety or depression in the context of future losses, because those losses will hark back—unconsciously—to the unresolved grief in his home when he was four.

And here's another problem: when these children become adults who experience panic disorder or major depression or trouble with intimacy, there is a good chance they will again be treated with medicine alone—maybe Paxil this time, or Effexor, or Lexapro, or Ativan, or Lunesta, or Depakote, or two or three combined.

And it isn't just medicine we turn to in order to keep underground the internal conflicts we ultimately need to dig up and resolve. We turn up our iPods, tuning out the world and quieting the nagging internal voices that tell us we are leading inauthentic lives. We obsessively dial our cell phones instead of dialing into our emotional realities. We connect to the Internet instead of to our core feelings about whether we were or were not well-loved as children. We lose ourselves in books such as *The Power of Now* that cleave us from the lessons of our own life stories by making the dangerous claim that past suffering should be ignored in favor of a pure focus on the moment.

Twelve-step programs such as AA and NA take up the noble task of getting addicts through sobriety one day at a time, but then let them down by railing against attempts to break all the way through their denial and unearth the emotional roots of their alcoholism, drug dependence, sexual addictions, overeating, or compulsive gambling.

Many psychologists even assert (based on spurious studies) that introspection could be a trap, snarling people in past crises when they could simply learn to ignore their histories and adopt a more positive mental outlook. Their argument could be summarized this way: the examined life is *not* worth living.

These are dangerous lies. Ignoring the facts of one's life— especially the painful ones—only puts the negative patterns unconsciously fueled by these issues more in command of one's future.

As Carl Jung wrote, "That which we do not bring to consciousness appears in our lives as fate."

You can't outdistance the past. The truth always wins.

GETTING TO THE TRUTH

Where do we begin to search for our true selves? For many people, the truth of their lives is a complete mystery. Unraveling most mysteries—especially those at the very heart of our life stories—creates confusion, at first. Confusion always precedes clarity.

Just think about the old detective series *Columbo,* starring Peter Falk. Columbo always ended up scratching his head in front of suspects, saying things like, "See, I'm confused about something you told me yesterday." Or "I'm still trying to make sense of this timeline, and I can't." He never let his confusion stop him. He took it as a sign that he should dig deeper for the truth.

Digging deeper for the truth begins like this: you start by identifying what trouble needs healing in your life right now, then you journey back into your life story to see the early conflicts that set the stage for it. Your vision will be clear only if you look directly and deeply into your pain, never away from it. And the lessons you learn from the difficult things you've lived through—your buried treasure—will free you to pursue a romantic relationship that isn't a replay of past relationships; a marriage untainted by unconscious, toxic lessons from your parents' marriage; a relationship with your children that isn't held hostage to unresolved dynamics from your own childhood; or perhaps a job that truly speaks to your heart.

Step 1: Focus on What's Wrong

Honestly assess up to three problems that motivated you to read this book, and write them down below (or in your notebook). Was it because of a stressful marriage? An addiction? A falling out with a best friend? A strained relationship with a parent? A sense of being powerless in the world? Or was it a combination of many different factors?

Your motivation for reading *Living the Truth* is crucial. It helps you identify what you need to address right now in order to live a more powerful life. It also helps you identify what part of your past you need to look at most closely. In this chapter, you have seen examples of what can happen when you underestimate the problems you face. Don't hold back and deny what's wrong. Writing all of it down is the first step to recognizing it and changing it.

I chose to read Living the Truth *because:*
(*Example:* "*I chose to read* Living the Truth *because* I need to change my stressful marriage.")

1. _____

2. _____

3. _____

Step 2: Focus on What's Really Wrong

For each part of your life that you feel you need to change, focus in on the specific aspect of it that troubles you. For instance, if you had written the example above — "*I chose to read* Living the Truth *because I need to change my stressful marriage*" — then you would really struggle to define what's stressful about it. Is it without passion? Is it marred by uncontrollable jealousy on the part of your spouse? Are you fed up with your spouse's infidelities? Are you being abused physically?

Your more focused response might be "*I chose to read* Living the Truth *because I need to change my stressful marriage, in which I can't trust my husband not to cheat.*" Another example might be *"I chose to read* Living the Truth *because I want to improve my marriage and bring back some of the passion we used to have."*

If your sentence reads *"I chose to read* Living the Truth *because I need to be less isolated from my family,"* then try to figure out why you've become isolated from them. Is it because you can't trust your parents to respect your boundaries? Is it because they always end up discouraging you from pursuing your dreams? Or is it because they so obviously favor your brother or sister over you? Your more focused response might now be *"I chose to read* Living the Truth *because I need to be less isolated from my family, in which I feel my sister gets all the attention."*

If your sentence reads *"I chose to read* Living the Truth *because I need to stop drinking,"* try to define whether low self-esteem, anxiety, or depression is fueling the addiction. Your response might now be *"I chose to read* Living the Truth *because I need to stop drinking, which I do to calm my anxiety about taking care of my family."*

Now rewrite your sentences, being as specific as possible about the problems.

I chose to read Living the Truth *because:*

1. _____

   _____

2. _____

   _____

3. _____

   _____

Right now, chances are that you, just like Nicole and Richard and countless others, are sitting with the untold truth that journeying into your life story—and truly revealing and accepting it—will yield the power that comes from feeling whole. The comforting distractions in your life—whether sugarcoated memories from childhood; on-again, off-again "love" affairs; or balms for low self-esteem such as compulsive eating or shopping or smoking or drinking too much alcohol—are depriving you of the personal riches that are the proper rewards of genuine self-knowledge.

The authenticity that comes with editing out the fiction from your existence will make you a better parent, husband or wife, lover or friend. It can utterly transform your life.

If you're like most people, the biggest thing that stands between you and your buried past is fear. You unconsciously believe that by looking squarely at what you have lived through, you could either lose yourself in the past or be overwhelmed by the truth.

I promise you that this will not be the case. You already possess the silver bullets to slay all the demons from your past.

How do I know? Because you have survived them. You are stronger than you believe. And by the end of this book, I will have proved that to you.

CHAPTER 2

Living Behind Shields

What happens when people live their lives trying to dodge the truth? It gets harder and harder to stop that truth from surfacing and slapping you hard in the face. You need to find ways to keep your mind from focusing on your pain. And that means alcoholism, drug dependence, addiction to food or gambling or cigarettes or sex, endless hours working jobs that don't speak to your heart because your heart is under wraps, romances that aren't true love because they're based on old lies, sons and daughters who can't connect with you because you aren't connected to your*self*.

And what a tragedy that disconnect really is. One of the reasons I love doing this work is that I'm convinced human beings are much more magical and moving than most of us know. The emotional defenses we use to obscure our personal truths end up obscuring the miraculous qualities that lie beneath those defenses: our God-given courage, compassion, devotion, trust, and—most important of all—capacity to love.

Our emotional vulnerability is itself a rare gift. Because without being vulnerable to sadness and disappointment and doubt, we would have no ability to truly experience and fully feel their opposites: joy, celebration, and reassurance.

Nobody wants to live in sadness, disappointment, and doubt. That's why all of us develop what I call "shield strategies" to keep emotional pain at bay. Some are fairly obvious, some much more subtle. But common to all shield strategies is the fact that they cover up the truth. And that truth—including every complicated, hidden, hurtful page of your life story—is your buried treasure. It is the nonfiction foundation upon which you can build real relationships, real character, real success, and real compassion for others.

You are the one holding the shield. And it only gets heavier with each passing day. It saps your energy. It steals your focus. And it cheats you of learning that you are far stronger, more courageous, and more capable than you believe. As long as you're holding the shield, you're living in fear.

Now imagine something else. Imagine that just beyond the shield, you're carrying a mirror. You can't see the mirror because the shield is in the way. But the mirror is capable of reflecting who you are and where you've been, going all the way back to your earliest years. It can show you how you have become the person you are today, why you continue to use self-defeating survival strategies you learned in childhood, and how you can make choices to change in dramatically positive and powerful ways.

Now envision that in order to start seeing the mirror that reflects the person you really are, you have to start putting down the shield. You don't have to drop it all at once, but you have to begin to lower it slowly.

The best way to go about this is to first identify the shield or shields you carry. Here are some of the more common ones:

- Overeating
- Overspending
- Obsessing over a romantic relationship
- Constantly arguing with your husband, wife, or partner
- Obsessing over dieting
- Obsessively exercising
- Sexual indiscretions or sexual addiction
- Perfectionism
- Staying online for hours
- Addiction to pornography
- Gambling
- Cigarettes
- Alcohol
- Drugs

One or more of these shield strategies may be the reason you bought this book to begin with. And you may have assumed that your perfectionism or gambling or smoking was an isolated problem. But shield strategies always mask deeper pain. They're all ways to create distractions. They take so much of your time and emotional energy that they prevent you from addressing core problems from the past that are actually fueling them. They're shield strategies you've been using to block the mirror you've feared looking into, the one that will let you see your true self, including the challenges you have survived, so you can make changes that are real and life-altering.

Nicole's shields included perfectionism, drinking too much, and shopping too often. What shields are you carrying? Take a few minutes right now to think about it. Then keep coming back to the question over the next hour or two, until you feel you have a real answer. Don't be afraid to add to your answer or to change it tomorrow or the next day or any time you feel you've gained more clarity.

My shield strategy is:
(*Example:* "*My shield strategy is* staying on the computer for hours at a time.")

1. _____

2. _____

3. _____

4. _____

5. _____

6. _____

It's also important to keep in mind that nearly every one of us bolsters his or her main shield strategies with very common behaviors. Watching television shows that shift your focus to fictional dramas rather than the real ones you've lived through; blaring music on the way to work and at the gym to keep your mind occupied; running yourself ragged with errands and invites; even flipping through one glossy magazine after another (instead of, say, flipping through family albums) are all ways to silence the internal "voice" that is continually trying to "read" your own life story to you. That voice speaks in unexpected memories and moments of insight that can start you on the path to living the truth—once you resolve to start listening.

LOWERING YOUR SHIELD

After you've identified your shield strategies, the next step is to begin to oppose them.

It would be wonderful if a two-packs-a-day smoker or an alcoholic were to quit right now, or a shopaholic were never to visit a mall or online store again, or a compulsive eater were to completely stop bingeing on food, or a workaholic were to suddenly cease the endless grind. But that isn't realistic for most people. And it isn't necessary. Living the truth starts with simply paying attention to your shield strategies more than before, noticing how often you use them, and then *beginning* to resist them.

Even simple changes—such as limiting television; wearing your iPod less frequently; sitting quietly and staring out the window for a few minutes during the day; thinking about the tough things you lived through as a child for ten minutes before dinner; looking through family photos from your childhood; reining in the clutter in your schedule to allow for a walk on the beach or in a park or down the street—will make it harder for your mind's defense mechanisms to defend against the truth.

The motivation to do so should be clear now. If you lower your shield even a bit, the edge of the mirror becomes visible. Lower it a little more, and you can begin to see yourself in earnest. Every small victory—one less cigarette, one night spent in the peace and quiet of home instead of out chasing romance, one less drink—is a step in the direction of self-discipline, self-awareness, and genuine self-improvement.

Look back at your shield strategies and write down specific plans you can commit to in order to help you see yourself for the first time (e.g., limiting television to one hour per day, keeping the radio turned off on the way to work, or taking a fifteen-minute walk by yourself without your iPod). Think of it as the art of spending time with yourself. You can't find your own story, or your own truth, when you are simply unwilling to spend time with your own thoughts.

My antishield strategy is:
(*Example:* "*My antishield strategy is* limiting my time on the computer to one hour in the evening, after dinner.")

1. _____

2. _____

3. _____

4. _____

5. _____

6. _____

Remember, it isn't supposed to feel good when you start using antishield strategies. Getting stronger never does. The fact that you feel anxious or depressed or irritable when you try to stop buying clothes, or bingeing on sweets, or talking for hours with a friend about your love life, or cruising the Web until the early morning, is a sign that you are detoxing from the things that have been keeping you from your buried treasure, your personal truth.

The painful cravings that an alcoholic experiences when he stops drinking are good, not bad. The depression that often comes with quitting smoking is good, not bad. Even the loneliness and feelings of loss that can come from taking time off from an addictive relationship are good, not bad.

Your emotions, including the painful ones, won't destroy your life; they will help you come fully to life.

Pain needs to be felt, because this is the path to insight, power, and fulfillment.

MONITORING YOUR SHIELD STRATEGIES

One of the most challenging parts of lowering your shields, keeping them down, and not deploying new ones is being aware of them at any point in time. The human mind is so adept at keeping you from your painful truths that it can keep you from focusing on what's blocking them from view.

I worked with one patient who stopped compulsively overeating and got so caught up in shopping for new clothes, and then working extra hours to pay for them, that she began canceling our sessions together. Only when I pointed this out was she able to see the way her mind was using three new shields — compulsive shopping, building up debt, and working overtime — to trick her into avoiding the truth.

In order to anticipate, identify, and overcome the use of shield strategies (whether old or new), you need to keep track of them. This allows you to gauge your progress in using antishield strategies and to formulate new ones as need be. I advise you to make several copies of this page in order to chart your progress each week.

Week _____ (one, two, etc.)

	Intensity level
My shield strategies: (e.g., overeating, smoking, etc.)	(1–10, 1 being least)
_____	_____
_____	_____
_____	_____

	Success
My antishield strategies: (e.g., visit a nutritionist and follow a new diet)	(1–10, 1 being least)
_____	_____
_____	_____
_____	_____

	Intensity level
Emerging (newly deployed) shield strategies: (e.g., constantly playing video games)	(1–10, 1 being least)
_____	_____
_____	_____
_____	_____

	Success
New antishield strategies: (e.g., limit video game use to one hour per day)	(1–10, 1 being least)
_____	_____
_____	_____
_____	_____

THE MUSIC BEHIND THE DANCE
OF SHIELD STRATEGIES

Please remember as you work to rid yourself of shield strategies that they take their power exclusively from fear—the fear that you are not strong enough to face reality, that if your true life story were to enter your consciousness, you would be overwhelmed. That may have been true when you were a child, but it isn't anymore. Your shields have outlived their usefulness and become threats to your psychological well-being. They are limiting you from growing into the complete, courageous, confident person I know you can be.

As you free yourself from the burden of carrying so many shields, the self-defeating half-truths and untruths you have told yourself (or that others have told you) about your life will lose their footing in your soul. You will embrace both your capacity to suffer and your capacity to succeed. You will feel, perhaps for the first time, completely human, capable of caring deeply for yourself and those around you. Your God-given potential for spiritual power, self-love, and love for others will have nothing in its way.

CHAPTER 3

Understanding the Four Fictions

If you were to tell someone the story of your life, would you be honest from start to finish? Or would there be gaping holes? Would there be chapters you would want to hide—not only from others but from yourself as well?

Because we unconsciously (and even neurologically) treat the painful chapters of our lives as the enemy, nearly every one of us creates a life story that is partly fiction. We instinctively deal with hurt—whether resulting from the loss of loved ones, the imperfections of our parents' marriages or their love for us, psychological trauma, growing up poor, growing up in chaos, growing up with an alcoholic or drug-dependent parent—by denying it.

The first step in this denial is to put up our shields to deflect the slings and arrows of everyday reminders of the pain so that we may live our lives, however dysfunctionally. But hard as we may try, we can't totally forget about how we grew up.

We tell ourselves palatable tales about what we lived through and who we lived through it with. And the more painful the truth, the deeper we bury it.

Yet the parts of us that hurt are also the most genuine and potentially powerful. They are the most vulnerable because they are the most exquisitely real. They include our inborn capacities to love, to trust, to dream, to create, and to empathize with the pain of others. Finding them again is like finding buried treasure, but the search takes courage.

Is there a map that leads to this treasure? I believe there is. And the place to dig can be found by tracking the energy we expend to keep the treasure hidden.

In my opinion there are four areas of life in which our early injuries occur and, therefore, four fictions we use to keep the truth at bay. Maintaining these fictions consumes an extraordinary amount of psychological energy. And beneath these fictions lie enormous reservoirs of personal authenticity and interpersonal power. The four fictions are:

- Fiction about the self
- Fiction about the actions and intentions of others
- Fiction about one's economic, social, or cultural circumstances
- Fiction about what it means to be mortal

FICTION ABOUT THE SELF

For the most part, before we emerge from childhood or adolescence, we note that life has not given us every gift. We see that we are stronger in some areas and more vulnerable in others, whether those areas are physical, emotional, or intellectual. We may be more athletic but less intelligent than others. We may be less attractive but more outgoing. Or we may be attractive, outgoing, and athletic but may face special learning challenges. Some of us struggle in childhood with medical conditions such as asthma. Others, with physical handicaps. Still others, with mood disorders.

As socially competitive creatures, we feel a host of emotions when we compare ourselves to others, including admiration, envy, superiority, inferiority, pride, and shame. And since we also have imaginations, we measure ourselves not only against people we know but against idealized notions (some promoted by television, films, and advertising) of what we wish to be and what we believe the world wants us to be.

Many of us make peace with our strengths and weaknesses and come to feel satisfied with who we are. But if those around us make us feel self-conscious and defensive about our shortcomings, or if no one helps to foster our core strengths, self-esteem is harder to come by. Our energy may be devoted to covering up. We can literally spend our entire lives creating and trying to sustain elaborate fictions to hide from others—and, not uncommonly, from ourselves.

Frank was forty years old when his attorney sent him to see me for a psychiatric evaluation before he was to go on trial for assault and battery. It was the third time he had been arrested for a violent offense. He'd had words with another man at work, had sensed things were about to get physical, and had, as he put it, "hit first and hit hard." He hadn't stopped with one punch, though. He had left the other man barely conscious. The prosecutor was asking for five to seven years in state prison.

"I've done jail time before," Frank told me. "It's nothing I can't handle. But if there's something wrong with me you think a jury ought to know, I'm good with that, too."

Everything about Frank was hyperbolically aggressive. He seemed like an actor playing a gangster. His tone of voice and mannerisms were, in fact, nearly identical to those of Tony Soprano, the fictional Mafia kingpin featured on the HBO television series. His face was scarred from a knife fight years before. He had worked out and taken steroids to create a hulking physique. Of every patient I have ever sat with, he is the last one I would want to meet in a dark alley.

"Tell me something," I said. "Why the tough-guy routine?"

He looked at me askance. "Excuse me?"

"You look like you're wearing armor and you talk like you just stepped off the set of *The Sopranos*. I'm guessing that means someone hurt you pretty badly when you couldn't defend yourself—like when you were growing up."

"Way off, Doc," he said. He smiled. "I'm a quick study. I ain't been beaten down since I was sucker punched back in the second grade."

I was drawn magnetically to that comment. Whenever someone offers up a memory of childhood pain, especially in the context of telling me how strong he is, I assume there's much more pain where that came from.

"So tell me about second grade," I said.

"Are you kidding me?"

"No."

"C'mon, Sigmund. What does second grade got to do with me going to jail?"

"Maybe nothing," I said. "But I won't know until you tell me about it."

After a lot more prodding, he did. He told me he'd been bullied for not being able to read. And he told me what his father had done to toughen him up. He had made him fight one bully after another in the family's front yard until he was satisfied his son had enough courage never to run away from anyone. "It was no big deal," Frank said.

But it *was* a big deal. It's called "growing up with a sadistic father," and it's a good reason to start looking really tough really fast.

"What did you do with all your fear?" I asked.

"Buried it, fast," Frank said, pointing at his heart.

"That's what I'm getting at," I said. "It's still there. The Soprano routine—like telling me you're fine with going to jail for five years—is your way of hiding it."

"Hey, I maybe had to put on a little act out there in the yard with my dad," he said, "but I promise I'm not acting now. I'm not afraid of anything."

The truth is that Frank was no longer conscious he was acting. The fear of being made fun of and being victimized had driven him so deep into the role of tough guy that he was now completely lost in it.

Just think what Frank might have become if he had been in touch with his pain instead of an expert at burying it: a teacher, reaching out to kids with learning challenges; a guidance counselor, sticking up for bullied kids; a pediatrician, helping children "fight off" powerful diseases (the ultimate bullies).

Think of the romantic relationship with a truly empowering woman he might have enjoyed in place of the dozens of flings and hundreds of one-night stands he'd had with women turned on by his gangland connections.

Frank's pain could have been his power. But like so many of us, he had become convinced that the best way to deal with the train wreck behind him (being bullied, living with a father devoid of empathy, feeling frightened and inadequate) was to keep running, despite stumbling and falling down on the tracks again and again, bleeding more and more.

All that running made him ignore a critical fact: the wreck was behind him. What he needed to do was turn and look at it.

"You're sure you're not afraid of anything?" I asked him toward the end of the session.

"Doc," he said, "I been beaten, knifed, clubbed. I got people right now saying they want me dead. Doesn't even faze me. Nothing does."

"How about reading?" I asked him.

He laughed.

"Did you ever learn?"

"Of course." He shrugged. "A little." His tone was softer, with a hint of sadness in it and less "street." "I do good enough to get by," he said, even more quietly.

I looked into his eyes and saw real pain. I nodded, understanding. A forty-year-old gangster had come into my office, but so had a little boy unable to read who had never stopped running away from that fact, or the feelings of weakness and vulnerability that had come with it.

We're all running from something. And the irony is that the very thing we're running from can be our ultimate source of psychological strength, if we face it and feel it and let it bring out the best in us.

I met with Frank several more times and helped him to see that his shame at not being able to read, along with his father's cruelty, was the fuel for his explosive rage. That rage had taken over during the assault and battery he was arrested for. Another jail term was inevitable. But this time, Frank resolved to use his years in prison to learn to read and to finish his college education.

"I figure the only way I'm ever gonna stop using my fists," he told me, "is to start using my head."

Frank may have been tough on the outside, but on the inside he was full of fear and insecurity. He fought all his life (internally and externally) so that no one would ever find out how vulnerable he really was. All that got him, however, was time behind bars.

What are your "tough guy" defenses? When you think about your childhood, are there parts you tend to just skim over rather than face and confront? Like Frank, you may be surprised that you need to go all the way back to second grade to figure out where your current pain originated—but what better place to start?

Living the truth happens naturally as you begin to refuse to live a life of fiction. And the best way to do that is to bring closer to the surface painful realities from the past that you've buried.

To get started, answer the questions below, and the questions throughout the rest of this chapter, as honestly as you can. Come back to them again and again as you read this book, adding facts and gut feelings and editing out any falsehoods.

What's your favorite story about your childhood—the one you most like to tell when people ask about your early years?

_____

_____

_____

_____

What's your least favorite story about your childhood—the one that includes the last thing you'd want a friend, a lover, or your spouse to know?

_____

_____

_____

_____

What part of your life story as a child or young adult took the most strength to survive?

_____

_____

_____

_____

• • •

The impression Frank wanted to leave on everyone he met was how tough he was. Sandra, a forty-six-year-old woman going through a contentious divorce, felt it important to let me know how smart she was. She told me, within a few minutes of meeting me, that she had graduated from Harvard (she wore a Harvard class ring) and had landed a position at a major accounting firm. I noted her clothing: elegant and serious, with designer insignia in plain view.

When someone volunteers how strong or smart or lucky or wealthy he or she is, you begin to wonder why the person feels the need to tell you that.

"It's like I'm at war," she said. "I'm not sleeping. I'm not eating. I can't concentrate. I mean, I'm a Harvard grad. I work at one of the biggest accounting firms in the world. And I can't balance a set of books to save my life. *I'm* out of balance. This divorce has taken over my life."

"Why is the divorce so bitter?" I asked Sandra.

"It wasn't at the beginning," she told me. "We were using a mediator to split our assets down the middle and set up joint custody of our two kids. When that didn't work, we went out and got killer lawyers."

"Who gave up on mediation first?"

"I did. I had no choice."

"What happened?"

"My husband owns a manufacturing company that's worth at least thirty percent more than he was claiming it was," she said. "The way he was valuing it made no sense whatsoever. And he knew it. But he had the gall to just say, 'Hey, you're okay with this, right?' Like I'm an idiot. I called a lawyer five minutes later."

"Your 'killer' lawyer," I said. "You were really angry."

"Beyond angry."

"Did you try to convince the mediator your husband was lying?"

"Why bother?" she said. Every trace of indecision, anxiety, and sadness left her voice. "I don't like being made a fool of."

Who does? But Sandra hadn't even tried to use her considerable skills as an accountant to get a fair settlement. "Do people generally think they can pull the wool over your eyes?" I asked. "You're obviously very smart, and your education speaks for itself."

"Nobody really goes there anymore," she said. "Maybe that's why I reacted the way I did when he tried."

Anymore. "Who *used to* 'go there'?" I asked.

She laughed. "No one. I mean, not since my brothers."

"Your brothers?"

"Trust me: it's ancient history. It's nothing, really."

It's no big deal. It's nothing. It's ancient history. These are self-soothing phrases people use to try to talk themselves out of their pain. "Tell me anyhow," I said.

Sandra suddenly *looked* pained. "It was just kid stuff. They're both smarter than I am . . . by a lot. They were constantly setting me up to take the fall for them with my dad. He was pretty strict."

"Setting you up . . . how?"

"Blaming me for every dumb thing they did. Leaving toys outside. The house being a mess. They stole money from his wallet once and put it in my room."

"Your dad didn't know they were lying?" I asked.

She shook her head. "They were good. It got to where *I* didn't know who was lying. I remember thinking, 'Wait, maybe I did forget to lock the front door.' 'Maybe I took money from his wallet by accident somehow.'"

Was it any accident Sandra had gravitated toward a career in which everything needed to add up? Was it any accident she had alerted me right away to her educational and professional credentials (her ability to reason and to defend herself intellectually)? And was it any surprise she had had a powerfully negative reaction to "being made a fool of" during her divorce mediation?

I wondered how closely the current situation mimicked the times during her childhood when she'd tried to explain the truth to her strict father. "Was your mediator a man?" I asked.

"Yes," Sandra said. "Why?"

"Older than you?"

"Much. A retired judge, like a lot of them. He had to be my father's age, at least."

Many mediators are retired male judges. And I don't want to make too much of Sandra mentioning her father in describing the one who'd been handling her divorce. But how much of a stretch is it to wonder whether her husband's lying during her mediation had brought Sandra too close to memories of her brothers lying to her father? How much of a stretch is it to wonder whether she unconsciously assumed a male mediator would dispense justice no more reliably than her dad?

Sandra's unresolved pain at being an easy mark for her brothers seemed not only to be involved in her holding forth a shield of credentials but to have short-circuited a mediation process she might otherwise have been able to use effectively, sparing her the emotional and financial costs of a protracted legal battle.

Had Sandra been living the truth, she might have addressed the mediator this way: "I hope you'll understand that when my husband feels free to present figures that so clearly undervalue his business, it makes me wary of trusting this process. If I seem upset, that's why. Having the wool pulled over my eyes—especially by someone I've shared so much of my life with—is very painful for me."

If Sandra had expressed her vulnerability instead of flashing her Harvard credentials, she would have stood a much better chance of encouraging the mediator to be fair to her. But Sandra hadn't been able to show her vulnerability. She was busy *covering it up*, acting more like the girl she was at home with her brothers and father than the woman she had become in the world.

What are the qualities you struggle most to make sure people know about you? (Your intelligence? Your physical strength? How many friends you have?)

_____

_____

_____

Why are these qualities so important to you? Complete the sentence below:
(Examples: "I want people to know how smart I am because my father always thought I was pretty but 'not too bright.'" *"I want people to know how well-liked I am because I was so unpopular in high school.")*
I want people to know how _____ *I am because:*

_____

_____

_____

I want people to know how _____ *I am because:*

_____

_____

_____

I want people to know how _____ *I am because:*

_____

_____

_____

FICTION ABOUT THE ACTIONS
AND INTENTIONS OF OTHERS

As difficult as it sometimes is to see the truth about ourselves, it can be just as—or even more—difficult to see the truth about others, especially those we love.

No one grows up with perfect parents and siblings and friends and teachers. But if the actions of others threaten our emotional or physical well-being when we are young, we may deny that fact and do whatever we can to see them in a reassuring light. And that can make it hard to find genuine love as an adult. We find the false "love" that we accepted as children. This dynamic is at the heart of painful conflicts in the lives of many of my patients.

Anne was twenty-nine when she came to see me, and in tears within a minute of sitting down. "I'm torturing myself," she told me.

"How so?" I asked.

"I think I'm just about the worst person in the world. I feel guilty constantly."

"About what?"

"I can't even believe I'm sitting here." She wiped away her tears. "I'm having an affair."

"How long have you been married?" I asked.

"Three years," she said. "And here's the really weird thing: I love Matt, my husband—at least I *think* I do. I know for sure I don't want to leave him."

"Tell me about him," I said.

"He's smart, handsome, supportive. I run a gallery that hasn't always made a lot of money, and he's been there for me from the minute we got engaged. I have this incredible safety net because of him, which only makes what I'm doing that much worse."

"Are you attracted to him?" I asked.

"We've always had phenomenal sex," she said. "That hasn't changed."

"What has?"

"Nothing has, actually. All we have is a physical connection. I don't think we connect emotionally at all."

"Why do you say that?"

"Because since I met Jason, I feel like I have a soul mate. I've never felt that with my husband."

"How did you meet Jason?" I asked.

"He bought a painting from me," she said. "My favorite one in the whole gallery. We started talking about the artist, then about art in general, then about . . . everything. We've never really stopped."

"Why do you think you married a man you didn't connect with emotionally?" I asked Anne.

"Got me."

"Is there anyone else you feel connected with other than Jason?"

"My mom, if that counts."

"The two of you are close?"

"To put it mildly," Anne said. "We talk two, three times a day."

"Have you told her about him?" I asked.

Anne blushed. She looked embarrassed, more like a little girl than a woman. "He's the only thing in my life she doesn't know about," she said.

As I talked longer with Anne, I realized that that was literally the truth. Her mother knew everything else about her. Anne checked in with her mother to tell her what she was wearing, how her day was going, if she made a sale at the gallery, if she and Matt argued, if they made up, what they were having for dinner at home, or where they were going out. It had always been that way, as long as she could remember. The close emotional bond between Anne and her mom had, in fact, made it very difficult for Anne to transition to college, where she had experienced severe anxiety about being away from home. It had made it impossible for her to attend the graduate school in Paris where she had been admitted to study art history.

"Does your mother approve of your husband?" I asked.

"She loves him," Anne said. "She thinks he's the perfect man for me." She paused. "Jason, she would hate. She's always said how she can't stand men who ask a million questions about what you're thinking and feeling. She likes the strong, silent type."

"That describes your husband?"

"He's a rock."

That made sense. It sounded to me like Anne's mother enjoyed having Anne to herself. She would approve of anyone who demanded no part of her daughter's soul.

"Do you see yourself leaving your husband for Jason?" I asked Anne.

"I've thought of it. But I don't think I'd go through with it."

"Why not?"

"I just worry he could end up being really high maintenance, emotionally."

"And you don't have that kind of bandwith available," I said.

"It doesn't feel like I do." She paused, looking confused. "Why is that?"

Over time, Anne was able to answer that question herself, partly because her mother kept demanding to know what Anne was talking about in therapy, then made it plain she thought it was a bad idea for her to be in therapy at all. She literally became jealous of Anne's relationship with me.

"What's her problem?" Anne asked me a few sessions later. "It's like she's trying to get inside my head."

"No," I said. "It's worse than that. She's already there. That's probably why you never thought you needed an emotional connection with a man. You were already taken—by her."

Anne was silent for several seconds. "Which is why I was satisfied just to be with Matt physically?"

"Until now," I said.

"But why now?" she asked.

"Maybe because you haven't really liked feeling alone in your own home these past three years," I said. "Or maybe because another man snuck up on you at the gallery and climbed inside your head when you weren't really looking."

Eventually, Anne lowered the shield covering her relationship with her mother, looked into the mirror reflecting her life history, and saw that her mother hadn't ever been purely a source of warmth and security. Her mother was using her to feel less alone. Seeing that complexity took courage, because it made Anne feel angry at her mother even though she still thirsted for her mother's love. And while that conflict may have been impossible for her to resolve as a little girl, now she was strong enough to face it.

Anne slowly began breaking free. She limited her calls to her mother and cut back on the information she shared about her marriage. She decided to find out how her husband, Matt, would respond to her sharing more of her thoughts and feelings with *him* instead. And she learned that he wasn't just someone she liked having sex with; he was actually someone she liked talking with.

As Anne's interest in her marriage grew, her interest in Jason waned.

"I'll always feel something special for him," she told me, "but I can't keep seeing him."

"Why's that?" I asked.

"Because I'm married," she replied.

"You were married when you met him," I said.

"Yeah, but for the first time, I really *feel* like I am."

Do you have anything in common with Anne? Are you hiding the painful reality that, when you were much younger, someone close to you disappointed you? Perhaps the following exercise will help you discover some hidden truths.

The people I could most rely on as a child or young adult were:

_____

_____

_____

The people I wish had been more reliable when I was a child or young adult were:

_____

_____

_____

The individuals from the previous statement let me down by:

_____

_____

_____

_____

The exercises you've been completing throughout these pages have a single goal: to help you stop running from the painful chapters in your life story and start learning from them.

The moment you cease living fiction designed to obscure your pain and start living the truth, you will begin to feel stronger. This is because you will stop seeing your demons through the eyes of a child and will realize you have grown stronger than that which you fear.

FICTION ABOUT ONE'S ECONOMIC, SOCIAL, OR CULTURAL CIRCUMSTANCES

Our stories include not only powerful characters whose actions can change the way we see our lives but also economic, social, and cultural realities that affect us deeply. To the extent that we deny the pain of having grown up poor (or simply less well-off than relatives or kids from another part of town) or without access to education, or having experienced prejudice as a member of a minority race or religion, that pain still controls us.

Some people become obsessed with escaping their backgrounds, wholly dedicating themselves, for example, to achieving wealth, to the exclusion of forging genuine and loving relationships. Others, convinced they will never overcome adversity, consistently shy away from challenges that could propel them in new directions. Still others turn to alcohol or drugs.

One of my patients was a Chinese woman named Julie who had been adopted into a white family at age six. She felt so self-conscious growing up with white sisters and the white girls in her neighborhood that, as an adolescent and adult, she did everything she could to distance herself from her own culture. She chose only white friends. She refused her parents' offers to take her to visit China. She married a white man.

But avoiding her discomfort with her own race only meant that Julie had to deal with it later. When she was thirty-one, her husband threatened to leave her because she was unwilling to have children, not wanting a baby that resembled her.

In order to save her marriage, Julie had to confront the pain of feeling different, isolated, and afraid as a little girl.

The fictions we create only grow more powerful until we face them.

I have treated several gay men and women who were hiding their sexual orientations from their families, fearing they would be ostracized. Before they could overcome that fear, they needed to lower their shields enough to feel the pain of having grown up in repressive communities, with parents whose love had always been conditional. Only once they confronted that reality, so overwhelming in childhood, could they "outgrow" it and settle for nothing less than being loved for who they were.

I treated a man named Andrew who grew up in poverty and was so terrified of falling back into it that he kept working sixteen-hour days, neglecting his wife and children, long after he was extraordinarily wealthy. In order to live a more balanced life, he had to confront how much fear and humiliation he had experienced as a boy, when he didn't have enough to eat or decent clothes to wear. Confronting that suffering allowed him to see that it was part of his *past,* when he was a child with no resources to change his circumstances. Now, as an adult with business skills, a history of great achievement, and vast financial resources, he had nothing to be afraid of. It just *felt* that way.

Harry Crews, one of my favorite authors, wrote eloquently in his collection of short stories *Blood and Grits* of his own resistance to accepting the pain of the early chapters of his life story. It took him decades to learn that that pain—from economic and social realities he grew up with—was truly his power.

I was sitting in a tiny room at the typewriter, trying not to wake up my eight-year-old son. Beside me in boxes were manuscripts. All rejected. Rejected because they were no good. I'd written ten years, and not a word had seen print. The room was filled with a palpable despair . . .

I was a twenty-four-karat fake; that was the trouble . . .

For many and complicated reasons, circumstances had collaborated to make me ashamed that I was a tenant farmer's son. As weak and warped as it is, and as difficult as it is even now to admit it, I was so humiliated by the fact that I was from the edge of the Okefenokee Swamp in the worst hookworm and rickets part of Georgia I could not bear to think of it, and worse to believe it. Everything I had written had been out of a fear and loathing for what I was and who I was. It was all out of an effort to pretend otherwise. I believe to this day, and will always believe, that in that moment I literally saved my life, because the next thought—and it was more than a thought, it was dead-solid conviction—was that all I had going for me in the world or would ever have was that swamp, all those goddamn mules, all those screwworms that I'd dug out of pigs and all the other beautiful and dreadful and sorry circumstances that had made me the Grit I am and will always be. Once I realized that the way I saw the world and man's condition in it would always be exactly and inevitably shaped by everything which up to that moment had only shamed me, once I realized that, I was home free. Since that time I have found myself perpetually fascinating. It wasn't many weeks before I loved myself endlessly and profoundly. I have found no other such love anywhere in the world, nor do I expect to.

Were there any economic, social, or cultural circumstances of your youth that were painful to you? List them here.

_____

_____

_____

What have you done to cover up or compensate for those circumstances (e.g., living to make money, like Andrew, because you grew up poor or denying your own roots, like Julie, because they made you feel different from others around you)?

_____

_____

_____

_____

_____

_____

When you cover up your pain, you also cover up your capacity to love yourself and others—a gift that can come only from feeling your pain and then sharing it. You cannot be the best person, parent, friend, or lover if you are pretending to be something you are not, guarding the vulnerable places in your soul. These are the very places to which others will connect most powerfully.

Isn't it time you started living the truth?

FICTION ABOUT WHAT IT MEANS TO BE MORTAL

Perhaps no fear is more universal and more universally denied than the fear of death. All of us will eventually have to say good-bye to those we love—when either their lives end or ours do. Yet most of us are loath to accept this reality. As the philosopher Ernest Becker wrote in his book *The Denial of Death*:

> Everything that man does . . . is an attempt to deny and overcome his grotesque fate [his eventual death]. He literally drives himself into a blind obliviousness with social games, psychological tricks, personal pre-occupations so far removed from the reality of his situation that they are forms of madness—agreed madness, shared madness, disguised and dignified madness, but madness all the same.

We refuse to feel the pain of being mortal. We *act* as though we have unlimited time to pursue our dreams or tell those we love exactly how we feel, or make amends to those we hurt, or make peace with those with whom we are in conflict. We have endless petty arguments with husbands and wives and children and friends and lovers whose loss would cut us to the core. But perhaps most of all, we act as though there is no urgency to unravel the mysteries of our own life stories, to live examined lives.

Nothing could be farther from the truth. We can't know how long we have to find our buried treasure and achieve personal authenticity. And there is no painless road to that invaluable goal, because we are at least as much what we have suffered through as what we have succeeded at.

You have this book in hand right *now*. It gives you the power and the path, if you have the courage, to stop living a fictional life and start living a real one. That means having the chance to identify your *real* talents, pursue your *real* goals, experience *real* well-being, and find *real* love. And if no one else has told you, I might as well be the first: you don't have forever.

CHAPTER 4

The Four Faces of Pain

As much as we try to shield ourselves from the painful events and themes in our lives, or to create fictional histories for ourselves, there's one important fact to remember: the pain doesn't go away. It doesn't disappear when we turn our backs on it. It is transmuted into other kinds of suffering, often very severe.

I call this principle the "preservation of pain"—when we don't deal with our original injuries, they crop up in other guises. In this sense emotional pain is no different from most physical pain. It is symptomatic of an original underlying problem. For example, what happens if you ignore the pain in your foot caused by a bone spur? You can shift your weight and adjust the way you walk to try to avoid the pain, but doing so is likely to cause serious issues down the road: knee, hip, and back pain; muscle spasms; joint erosion; possibly even broken bones and head trauma, should your "defensive" way of walking end up making you fall down again and again.

When emotional pain is repressed, the results can be much

more wide-ranging, even life-threatening. They include one or more of the *four faces of pain:*

- Interpersonal conflicts
- Physical illnesses
- Pathological behaviors
- Psychiatric disturbances

REPRESSED EMOTIONAL PAIN AND INTERPERSONAL CONFLICTS

Our communications with one another are colored by our histories. We bring to each moment every significant experience and relationship we have ever had, whether we are conscious of the psychological lessons they taught us or not.

Unfortunately, the most painful lessons are the ones we are least likely to fully examine. And that means they are the *most* likely to grow powerful underground roots and contaminate our attempts to build new relationships on trust, mutual respect, and love.

When your own history is not clear to you, the pages are not bound in place by understanding and can therefore insert themselves anywhere in your life story. Then you have little capacity to separate the present from the past, and the painful relationships you have lived through long ago will bring you into conflict with others over and over again.

Conflict is itself one of the most magnetic forces in the universe. An unexamined life leads to chronic conflict, because human beings gravitate naturally to it.

Ask any accomplished screenwriter or novelist, and he or she will tell you that people watching a film or reading literature are irresistibly drawn to the parts of the story in which one character's goals or feelings or actions are in direct opposition to those of another: a daughter wants to marry a man her parents disapprove of; a lawyer defends a client that his partner is dead-set against him representing; a wife threatens to leave her boxer husband if he takes that last fight; an investment banker must decide whether to make a deal that would enrich his firm but violate the ethics of his father.

No one would go to see a film about a very nice woman and very nice man who meet, treat each other with respect, celebrate their growing love, and share their boundless happiness with their very supportive families. Our emotions are not engaged nearly enough to pay money to watch that lovely story.

Because we are drawn to the high-energy dynamics of conflict, we will automatically introduce our unresolved guilt, anger, fear, sadness, disappointment, or jealousy from prior, often very early, relationships into new relationships. And what's more, we will seek out people who can bring their own conflicts to the table, to drive the energy level yet higher.

Those who maintain they are "conflict-averse" and "can't stand arguing" are actually *more* likely to invite conflict into their lives. This is because their tendency to run away or turn the other cheek when they should be standing their ground ends up attracting bullies and predators.

It takes being comfortable with conflict—not being drawn to it or afraid of it—to minimize its role in one's life.

A patient of mine named Mary comes to mind. Mary was forty-six years old when her husband of twenty-two years, an extremely controlling man on whom she had depended for nearly everything, died. Since the couple had no children, she decided to move from her small town outside New York into the city.

Without the "safety" of the dependent relationship she had had with her husband (never having had her own bank account, for example), Mary engaged in a string of painful relationships over the course of several months. One person after another—a new female friend, a man she had begun to date, a contractor working on her apartment, a lawyer settling her husband's estate and finalizing the sale of her home in the suburbs—seemed intent on taking advantage of her. Her friend asked to borrow money for a week and never made any attempt to repay her. Her new boyfriend told her he was in love with her, slept with her several times, then moved on without explanation. Her contractor overcharged her and delivered poor service. And her lawyer demanded a sizable retainer, was generally unavailable to her, and did a poor job of protecting her husband's assets from estate taxes.

Mary came to me with low mood and low self-esteem, wanting to know whether she was a "magnet" for abusive people. She intuited she wasn't just having bad luck; she worried she might be making her own bad luck.

When I spoke with Mary, it became evident that she had indeed invited people to be irresponsible and untrustworthy toward her. She had disclosed the sizable amount of her inheritance to her new "friend" during the first lunch the two of them shared. She insisted on picking up the tab for that lunch and several more. She "pushed" her friend to take the loan that the woman never repaid. The first time she met her new "boyfriend," she told him how lonely she felt and how she was sexually inexperienced. She paid her contractor in full, in cash, before he started work. And she not only forgot to ask for a retainer letter from her attorney but told him she was entirely in his hands because she had no financial expertise whatsoever.

Mary had positioned herself as a potential victim again and again. The question was, why? What in Mary's past would have led her to marry a controlling man, remain in a marriage in which she was powerless for twenty-two years, and then unconsciously choose one person after another with the predisposition to take advantage of her (not to mention giving them ample opportunity to do so)?

The answer (no surprise) went back to her childhood. After spending more time with Mary and gaining her trust, I learned that her mother had died when she was just two years old, leaving her with her father, a man who had very little interest in Mary's thoughts or ideas and had a bad habit of not turning up at her dance recitals or gymnastics meets or even graduations. The only thing Mary could truly rely on her father for was to be very kind to her whenever she was frightened or sad or ill. Her father, her sole support in the world, responded best to her when she showed weakness.

Mary had never outgrown the fear that leading with strength would leave her alone in the world. When she married, her husband replaced her father as the one who embraced her wholeheartedly when she was needy but never when she was strong. And if Mary ever thought of leaving him, she was kept in check by the deeply buried, powerful fear of a little girl who had lost her mother and couldn't risk separating from her dad.

Learning From the Past

Robert Pirsig, author of *Zen and the Art of Motorcycle Maintenance,* wrote: "What sort of future is coming up from behind I don't really know. But the past, spread out ahead, dominates everything in sight."

Once Mary and I made the connection between buried pain from her past and the interpersonal conflicts with which she was struggling in the present, she began to notice how often she described herself as foolish or helpless or "out of it." She remembered many other times she had been hurt by people after "inviting" them to take advantage of her.

She started to take notice of all the instances in a single day she portrayed herself as weak. Stopping her routine of helplessness, however, took practice and didn't feel normal right away. She wasn't used to being treated as anyone's equal and wasn't sure how to stay on a par with others and still connect with them and inspire them to care about her.

She persevered. She started to speak more about "surviving" the loss of her husband than feeling "devastated" by it. She stopped describing the idea of taking over her own finances as "hopeless" and started describing it as "something worth sinking her teeth into."

Linking the past with the present, together with using the language of hope and power, not only made Mary *feel* more powerful but also made her *act* that way. She took much more control of the legal process surrounding her husband's estate. She told contractors her "expectations" of them rather than saying she desperately needed their help. She refrained from informing a new love interest that she was "lonely," instead telling him that she would *rather* be lonely than in a bad relationship. And she learned that these people didn't end up abandoning her; they simply had more respect for her.

Any time you meet someone new, keep in mind that you are meeting someone whose thoughts and actions are partly based on his or her life history, not just his or her history with you. To the extent that that person has not faced the interpersonal struggles he or she has lived through, those struggles will be reborn in every new relationship he or she forms.

The same is true for you.

When I was a medical student completing my rotation on the infectious disease service, I helped to treat a roughly sixty-year-old man who had been admitted to the hospital with pneumonia. He told me he was about to get divorced for the fifth time. When I asked him what he had learned about marriage, he smiled. "I'm not sure I've learned a thing," he said. "All I can tell you is that with the first four, you swear it's *their* fault."

That was a good insight, if a little late in coming. It signaled the man's recognition that four women hadn't conspired to fill so many chapters of his life with conflict. He'd been the coauthor of each and every one of those chapters. The next step would have been for him to identify what painful, unexamined dynamic from his past kept pulling him back into the same self-destructive orbit. He would have needed to find the courage to dig up his buried treasure and start living the truth.

None of us is condemned to live a life mired in interpersonal conflict, revisiting our pain again and again. We can overcome our pain once and for all, revolutionizing our friendships, business partnerships, romances, and marriages. We just have to be willing to face it and feel it.

REPRESSED EMOTIONAL PAIN AND PHYSICAL ILLNESSES

The conflicts that we have in life aren't always with other people. Sometimes we focus those conflicts inward and, with no other outlet for our emotions, unconsciously cause ourselves to produce physical symptoms or to experience real physical harm.

One of the chief ways repressed psychological pain manifests itself is through physical pain. Tension headaches, migraines, backaches, and recurrent (and sometimes severe) abdominal distress all have recognized links to unresolved emotional suffering.

Remember when you were a child and something was troubling you? How did you express yourself? Often, no doubt, you did so through physical symptoms. You told your parents you had a headache or your tummy hurt. And it did. Because unresolved emotions, including worry and shame and anger, can literally *hurt*. In adulthood, they have the capacity to cause painful muscle contractions in the head, neck, stomach, and lower back. And in a similar way, overactivity of the smooth muscle that lines blood vessels and the GI tract can translate into hypertension, heart disease, and gastroesophageal reflux disease.

We all understand at a basic, intuitive level that putting words to one's unspoken, buried emotions diminishes their power to wreak havoc with our bodies. That's why, when you had an unexplained stomachache or headache, your mother probably asked, "Are you worried about anything? Is anything bothering you at school? With your friends? You can tell me." She wasn't only concerned that you might be hiding your distress *from her.* She was also worried that you could be hiding it *from yourself* and trying to deny it, therefore causing physical symptoms.

Adults need to put words to their repressed emotional suffering, too, because the physical toll of not doing so only gets greater as we age.

More than ever before, scientists are acknowledging that stress and repressed anger and unacknowledged grief are linked to a wide array of physical illnesses. Now, with the emergence of a field called *psychoneuroimmunology,* comes the realization that our minds, our brains, and our immune systems influence one another in much more powerful ways than we ever knew.

Gabor Maté, MD, makes the connection clear in his book *When the Body Says No:*

> Physiologically, emotions are themselves electrical, chemical, and hormonal discharges of the human nervous system. Emotions influence—and are influenced by—the functioning of our major organs, the integrity of our immune defenses, and the workings of the many circulating biological substances that help govern the body's physical states. When emotions are repressed . . . this inhibition disarms the body's defenses against illness. Repression—dissociating emotions from awareness and relegating them to the unconscious realm—disorganizes and confuses our physiological defenses so that in some people these defenses go awry, becoming the destroyers of health rather than its protectors.

Indeed, research has established that one of the major risk factors for autoimmune diseases such as rheumatoid arthritis, lupus, and multiple sclerosis, in which the body's own defenses attack healthy tissues, is stoicism, a personality stance in which pain is neither explored nor expressed.

Autoimmune disorders are just the beginning, though. Maté cites data from the National Cancer Institute showing that natural killer cells—immune cells in the body capable of destroying cancer cells—function better in breast-cancer patients who are able to express anger than in those adept at burying it. And he cites other studies that suggest women are at greater risk of developing breast cancer if during their childhoods they learned to repress their emotions. One research study Maté identifies has found that women are at greatest risk if they display "emotional disconnection from their parents or other disturbances in their upbringing; if they tend to repress emotions, particularly anger; if they lack nurturing social relationships in adulthood; and if they are altruistic, compulsively caregiving types." (Wirsching, M. 1982. Psychological identification of breast cancer patients before biopsy. *Journal of Psychosomatic Research* 26. Cited in Cooper, Cary L., ed. 1993. *Stress and Breast Cancer.* New York: John Wiley and Sons, Bahnson, C. B. 1981. Stress and cancer: The state of the art. *Psychosomatics* 22:213.)

Still not convinced? Maté also presents data from a decades-old study by British chest surgeon David Kissen showing that patients with lung cancer often turn out to have lifelong patterns of not expressing their emotions. For example, men who lack the ability to talk about their feelings are at five times greater risk than those who can express themselves.

Kissen's findings were supported by a study conducted over a ten-year span in a small town of about fourteen thousand called Crvenka in former Yugoslavia. Researchers followed about fourteen hundred men and women to see what risk factors were linked to various diseases. As Maté writes:

By 1976, ten years later, over six hundred of the study participants had died of cancer, heart disease, stroke, or other causes. The single greatest risk factor for death—and especially for cancer death—was what the researchers called rationality and anti-emotionality, or R/A.

The researchers wrote, "Indeed, cancer incidence was some forty times higher in those who answered positively to ten or eleven questions for R/A [showing they habitually repressed their feelings] than in the remaining subjects, who answered positively to about three questions on average."

Being willing to confront the truth about your life story, to face your pain and express what you feel, can not only change your life but literally save it.

When Physical Pain Can't Be Explained

Emotional pain doesn't have to be buried for many years to cause physical symptoms. Back in 1991, toward the end of my training in psychiatry, I treated a seventy-one-year-old woman named Naomi who was referred to me because her feet burned relentlessly. The pain was so severe that there were days she couldn't walk and spent hours lying in bed, in tears. Her internist had performed a full physical exam and run all the laboratory studies she could think of but couldn't find any reason for Naomi's pain. MRI, CT, and ultrasound examinations all came back normal. A neurologist had performed nerve conduction studies, and a vascular surgeon had performed an angiogram. Both showed no problem whatsoever.

Naomi had trouble concentrating when she met with me the first few times because her pain was so severe. She closed her eyes again and again and buried her frail hands in her hair. I had the sense that it was very important for me to sit through some of that pain with her, supporting her and comforting her to the extent that I could, so she would understand that I knew her pain was real—even though her other doctors had given her the sense they doubted it.

It wasn't until our third session (one week after I had started Naomi on a low dose of an antidepressant) that Naomi said the first thing that invited me to begin exploring the real source of her suffering. Just moments after sitting down in my office, she said, "You know, you look a little like my grandson." She smiled weakly. "More than just a little, to tell you the truth. I don't know how I could have missed it until now."

Although she didn't know it, Naomi had just given me an important insight into her condition. When someone wonders how they could have missed something about a person or a situation, assume that's because it was too big to see (like a mountain viewed from a foot away), not too small.

"Tell me about your grandson," I said.

She shrugged. "There's not a lot to tell. He's a wonderful boy. Very caring. Very smart. He writes to me every week."

"He lives out of state?" I asked, wondering if Naomi missed him.

"No, right here in Boston," she said. "He loves it here. He always tells me he'll be back to stay."

"Where is he?"

"Kuwait," she said.

1991 was, of course, the year of Operation Desert Storm, America's response (along with our allies) to the invasion of Kuwait by Iraq. Over 500,000 American troops were deployed to the Persian Gulf as part of the effort. Naomi's grandson was one of the troops.

Before my training in psychiatry, I might have been content to know Naomi had a grandson who reminded her of me and that he was not at home. I might have settled for the shorthand generalization that all grandmothers in Naomi's position would miss their grandsons, forgetting that no person's story is exactly the same as anyone else's. I might have wondered to myself whether missing him was making her pain worse. But I wouldn't have kept the wound open long enough to explore how deep it was and exactly where it led. That instinct had developed in me over the course of my residency, by meeting with patient after patient and by confronting my own wounds with my therapist, the late James Mann, MD.

"What else does he say in his letters?" I asked Naomi. "Is he scared?"

"He isn't scared," she said. "He's proud to be serving his country. The main thing that bothers him is the weather."

"What does he say about that?" I asked.

"He says it's very, very hot there," she said. "He says that the sand is like fire. No matter what boots he wears, his feet . . ."

Naomi and I both slowly looked down at her *feet*. The room was silent, the moment full of wonder. When I spoke, it was just above a whisper. "His feet burn," I said.

She shook her head. "You don't think . . ."

I took a few moments to collect my thoughts. "I think," I said, "that you love your grandson very, very much. And I think we should talk more about him."

We did. We talked for hours about Naomi's grandson's special talents, including his skills as an athlete. We talked about how important he was to her, since he was her only grandchild, Naomi having lost a granddaughter shortly after childbirth. And finally, we talked about her fear that he would never return from Kuwait, that he would die so far away from home.

If I ever doubt the power of love or the miracle of empathy, if I am ever tempted to believe that neuroscience holds every answer to human emotion and behavior, if I ever question whether an alchemy of the soul can change buried fear or anxiety or sadness into physical illness, I shall remember a grandmother I once met whose feet burned relentlessly for her grandson fighting in a distant desert.

Repressed emotional pain can *cause* physical illness. That

means that part of preventive medicine for every one of us has to be a psychological exploration of the very things we would *rather not explore*. Because if we don't summon the courage to find out what is fractured inside us, we may very well need to find the courage to live through the physical symptoms born of our fears.

REPRESSED EMOTIONAL PAIN AND PATHOLOGICAL BEHAVIORS

Once Naomi faced her pain and discovered its source, her symptoms slowly disappeared (and, thankfully, her grandson came home alive and well from Kuwait). Some people, however, are so determined to run from their pain that they will resort to a variety of behaviors designed to distract themselves from it or will literally anesthetize themselves. And because the only way to achieve emotional stability is to turn and face one's suffering, these attempts at avoidance will always cause one to suffer more, not less, in the long run. Remember my theory of "preservation of pain."

Perhaps the most common failed behavioral strategy to avoid pain is to begin abusing alcohol or illicit drugs. Every alcoholic or drug addict I have ever treated or whose care I have overseen has demonstrated a marked inability or unwillingness to confront the reality of his or her life story and explore its most painful chapters. The same is true for people who "need" two or three drinks to get through the day or forty doses of nicotine (from two packs of cigarettes) or a joint or narcotic "painkillers." They are literally choosing to use anesthesia on a frequent, often daily, basis in order to escape their pasts and *not* feel.

The toll of this running from pain is nearly incalculable — lost relationships, lost jobs, broken families, criminal records for driving under the influence, liver disease, neurological disorders, cancer — you name it.

Unfortunately, psychiatry's recent focus on using official diagnostic codes (e.g., *Diagnosis 303.90, Alcohol Dependence* or *Diagnosis 291.3, Alcohol-Induced Psychotic Disorder, with Hallucinations*) to label emotional suffering, rather than using empathy to understand it, encourages alcohol- and drug-dependent people to lose themselves in the "sick role." An anonymous illness, they can tell themselves, has them firmly in its grip. What they have lived through isn't linked to what they are suffering from now. You won't find any reference to soul-searching or moments of epiphany in the American Psychiatric Association's *Diagnostic and Statistical Manual of Mental Disorders, Fourth Edition.*

As already mentioned in chapter one, twelve-step programs such as Alcoholics Anonymous and Narcotics Anonymous run the risk of compounding the damage by reassuring alcoholics and drug abusers that they are "powerless" in the face of their illnesses and that religious faith, rather than determination to face pain, is the key to their well-being.

This "religious" philosophy neglects a critical link between faith and suffering. Every major religion acknowledges that it is through *facing* one's pain, rather than running away from it, that spiritual growth and emotional well-being become possible.

Esteemed Roman Catholic cardinal Désiré-Joseph Mercier (1851–1926) put it this way: "Suffering accepted and vanquished will . . . give you a serenity which may well prove the most exquisite fruit of your life."

Pope John Paul II wrote in a 1984 apostolic letter, "Salvifici Doloris" (The Christian Meaning of Human Suffering), "Christ leads into this world, into this Kingdom of the Father, suffering man, in a certain sense through the very heart of his suffering. For suffering cannot be *transformed* and changed by a grace from outside, but *from within.* And Christ through his own salvific suffering is very much present in every human suffering, and can act from within that suffering by the powers of his Spirit of truth, his consoling Spirit."

In the Old Testament, suffering is seen as the key to redemption. Isaiah made it clear that appalling disasters, *when confronted*, could be transmuted into spiritual triumphs.

Rumi, the philosopher and mystic of Islam, wrote, "No one possesses good fortune but he who takes to Him an aware spirit."

The motivating concept at the core of Buddhism is that all existence is suffering and that the path to spiritual enlightenment involves seeing—and feeling—that fact.

Grace, hope, and salvation are the just rewards of those who resolve to trust in God or life or themselves enough to unearth their buried treasures.

It isn't enough for alcoholics and those with drug dependencies to acknowledge weakness in the face of one substance or another. It isn't even enough for them to acknowledge the harm they have done to themselves and others by drinking or using drugs. What's really necessary to "cure" substance-dependent individuals is to unearth the roots of their dependencies, the reasons *why* they have sought to anesthetize themselves. It's necessary to dig deep into their life stories for the original injuries that caused the psychological pain from which they are fleeing.

Rather predictably, given our cultural aversion to feeling pain, the newest treatments for addiction utilize chemical tricks to either block an addictive substance from yielding its desired effect on the brain or fool the brain into thinking the substance is present when it isn't. Naltrexone, for example, displaces heroin from its chemical receptors in the nervous system, making it impossible for it to induce euphoria. Naltrexone also seems to interfere with the intoxicating effects of alcohol. Buprenorphine, on the other hand, mimics some of the effects of opiates but doesn't seem to cause as much craving. Methadone works the same way.

The trouble is that while these medicines are excellent tools to stabilize patients long enough to find out *why* they are dependent on substances, these treatments are now generally used (along with antidepressants such as Prozac, antianxiety agents such as Klonopin, and sleep aids such as Ambien) to help patients pretend they don't need to worry about the *why* of their addictions at all.

Detoxification is even available in a painless version that makes withdrawal unnoticeable because patients are under general anesthesia at the time.

Think about that: patients with an aversion to suffering, who have opted to fill their bodies with chemicals in order to *not feel,* can now be taken off those chemicals without feeling anything at all (because of stronger chemicals that render them completely unconscious).

No wonder the treatment is popular with addicts.

At the heart of this and all misguided clinical approaches to addiction is the belief that addicts have broken brains, not deep emotional wounds.

I know otherwise. Having been medical director of detox units and outpatient mental health clinics, and having treated many cocaine-, alcohol-, marijuana-, and heroin-dependent patients in my private practice for the past fifteen years, I am certain that in order to truly heal these individuals, a therapist must encourage them to confront the original source of the pain they are desperately trying to avoid. The therapist must literally help patients summon the *will* to reopen early chapters in their life stories that their minds have kept closed—out of fear.

Addicted to Guilt

Several years ago I treated a fifty-five-year-old man named Max who had been referred to me by a major university. Max had been an aeronautical engineering professor whose research laboratory specialized in jet engine propulsion. For many years, he had received military grants to help design new fighter planes.

Everyone at the university knew Max's work was his life. He used to tell his students that he lived, ate, and breathed aeronautical engineering. During the 1990s, however, defense spending decreased, Max's grants weren't renewed, and the university told him they couldn't afford to provide him with free lab space.

Max took a severance package, with benefits, and stopped working.

What no one knew was that Max had been drinking four to five beers a day while putting in twelve- to fifteen-hour days at the lab, seven days a week. Often, he wouldn't go home to his apartment at all, spending the night on the couch in his office.

Max had been married briefly but had no children. He had no outside interests. He had no friends. His work had been all-consuming to him, like a drug.

Without anything to keep his mind focused (and "safe" from revisiting the intense childhood pain he ultimately revealed to me), Max used more of the only other drug he knew: alcohol. He started drinking a six-pack a day, then switched from beer to whiskey. Within a few months, he was drunk most of the day, every day. He paid no attention to his bills or to keeping up his apartment. Finally, he was evicted and began living on the streets.

The trip from professor to homeless man had taken less than a hundred days.

The university continued to pay Max's medical insurance, which covered more than a dozen inpatient "detoxes" over the next few years. It covered over thirty emergency room visits for injuries Max sustained falling down on the street or getting beaten up in bars. It covered his treatment for repeated bouts of pancreatitis, a painful, potentially life-threatening inflammation of the pancreas caused by drinking.

Finally, the managed care representative at the insurance company, a former practicing psychologist, decided it was time to try to find out *why* Max was drinking. He called me and hired me to start meeting Max at restaurants and coffee shops to attempt to restore him to some acceptable level of functioning.

Max agreed to meet with me, in part because I agreed to pay for lunch.

When I first saw Max, I was taken aback by his appearance. I had naively thought he would look like a university professor with a hangover, maybe with a badly wrinkled shirt and a hole in the knee of one pant leg. But he looked like a bum. He had a three-day growth of beard, wild hair, a deep gash across the bridge of his nose, and bloodshot eyes that looked through me. He had had at least a few drinks and smelled like it. But he had shown up for our meeting, which told me he hadn't completely *given up*.

Max initially rejected the idea that there could be any connection between anything he had lived through as a child and what he was living through on the streets. He insisted that engineering was an objective discipline (and, hence, reliable) while psychiatry was a subjective one, closer to an art than a science (and, therefore, not reliable).

He was surprisingly easy to be with, partly because he was so intelligent, partly because he had kept his sense of humor, and partly because he was quick to end any period of silence by offering up a witty or controversial comment designed to spark another round of debate.

Max was such a good conversationalist, in fact, that I began to wonder how uncomfortable he was with silence. On a few occasions, I intentionally answered one of his questions with just a word or two. He was always right there to fill in the blanks and keep things moving.

For our first three lunches, I let our intellectual debates fill our time together. But during our fourth meeting, I nodded toward two little boys sitting with their parents at a booth nearby and asked Max why he had never had any children himself. The question had come naturally to me because I was in my mid-thirties at the time, Max was twenty years older, and something about the way he had listened patiently to my positions before debating them felt almost fatherly to me.

"I never liked kids," he said. "That's what ended it with my wife. She wanted a baby. I didn't."

"What bothers you about them?"

He shrugged. "They need too much," he said.

"Such as?" I asked.

"Food," he joked.

I smiled. "No, really," I said.

He shrugged. "Food is pretty important. Trust me, I know."

Max may have wanted me to think he was being funny, but it has become pretty clear to me that when someone repeats a joke after I've asked him to be serious, I should assume he wasn't joking to begin with.

"Did you grow up without enough to eat?" I asked.

He tried to appear as though he were more interested in getting the waiter to refill his coffee than the question on the table, but the effort was obvious. "My father made sure we never went hungry," he said, waving the waiter down.

"Was that hard for him at times?"

"You're working now," he said. He winked at me.

The waiter arrived with coffee and refilled our cups.

"Was it, though?" I persisted. "Was it hard for him to keep food on the table?"

"With five kids, trying to make money as a writer? Nah. It was a breeze."

I just kept looking at him.

"I think it was hard for him to do anything other than write," he said finally. "But he did what he had to do and never complained about it a single day in his life. He was too good for that." He looked away as his eyes filled up. "He was too good for any of us."

What Max's father had had to do, it turned out, was to give

up writing fiction—his passion—and go to work in a factory to support the family. He died just shy of retirement age, just before he could go back to doing what he loved to do in the world.

Max's life story—and the story of his drinking—suddenly made sense to me. Max had turned his life into an answer to his father's problem, deciding not to have a family and to devote himself exclusively to the work he loved.

The trouble was that when Max's work came to an end, he had nothing else in his life—other than alcohol.

What's more, after a few more lunches, I realized the work had *never* truly been enough for Max, even though he'd been spending nights in his lab. That's why he needed to drink four or five beers a day. He felt isolated and alone.

He also felt guilty. He saw himself as one of the reasons his father had never been able to fully pursue what he loved in the world. He saw himself as a burden.

"If he never told you that you stood between him and his writing," I asked, "how did you get the idea that you did?"

"He didn't have to tell me. I saw him get up plenty of mornings and try to get something down on paper before the sun even came up."

"He loved it," I said.

Max nodded.

I waited. "But he loved you more."

"Doesn't compute, Doctor," Max said. "He did what he had to do. He did the right thing. That's who he was."

"You don't give him enough credit," I said.

"I give him all the credit in the world."

"No one forced him to have a big family. He *wanted* one. He *chose* to put his work second. Just like you chose to put yours first."

Max didn't have a quick response. He looked directly at me.

"Creating you was more important to him than creating fiction."

"Some creation," Max said. He shook his head.

I decided it was time to take a firm stand. "Then do better," I said. "Because I'll tell you this: he wouldn't be happy at all to see how one of the stories he started to write—which happens to be *your* story—is turning out. I don't think it does much to honor the sacrifice he made."

Max looked at me for a few moments. He glanced at the children at the table nearby. Then he looked back at me. "You're saying I owe him something?"

"No," I told him. "That's what you're saying."

Max arrived at our next lunch, shaking, in a suit that needed pressing and a white shirt soaked through with sweat.

"What's wrong?" I asked him.

He could barely hold his coffee cup without dropping it. He managed to take a sip. "I'm going cold turkey," he said. "I'm all done. What we talked about last time . . . it sunk in."

"If you really want to be done," I said, "then you should do it the right way. Let me get you into detox again. If you're out on the streets and start feeling worse and worse, you're more likely to start drinking."

He shook his head. "I don't want to go in again."

"You mean," I said, "you want to drink again."

He thought about that. He struggled to take another sip of coffee and spilled some on his shirt. He looked down at the stain, then back at me. "You don't believe I can beat this on my own," he said.

"I don't believe there's any reason you should have to," I told him.

Max admitted himself later that day for yet another detox. He stayed sober only a few weeks after he was discharged. But this time, rather than spending months on the streets, he went right back into the hospital. When he got out, he managed to put together ninety days of sobriety. After a few more admissions, he stayed sober six months. He rented a small studio apartment, started Alcoholics Anonymous, and even began to talk about going back to work.

"I'm not saying I'm cured," he told me over lunch one day, "but things are definitely different now. I'm thinking differently."

"In what way?" I asked him.

"It's not just about me anymore. I don't want to let myself down, but I don't want to let you down either. And I sure as hell don't want to let my father down."

I really couldn't find anything to say that would add to those powerful words, so I said nothing.

"I'm also having really crazy thoughts," he said.

That sounded worrisome. "Such as?" I asked.

He laughed. "I'm thinking about going out on a date."

"A *date*." It felt strange even saying that word around Max. He had been so singularly focused on his work for so many years, then sick for so long, that I had never thought of him doing anything as commonplace as asking someone out to dinner or a movie. "Great idea," I said. "What made you think of it?"

He grew very serious. "I've been thinking about how much I miss my father and my mother," he said. "For the first time, I feel really, really lonely. And all of a sudden, I'm scared I could be alone forever."

Max was feeling lonely and scared, and that was good. Because he was finally able to put down his shields and start feeling, instead of working himself to the point of exhaustion or drinking himself into oblivion. Reopening the early chapters of his life history had unlocked the possibility of wonderful new chapters in the future. "Being scared of being alone," I said, "might be a decent insurance policy against it happening."

Two years later, Max was teaching engineering part-time at the university and living with a woman he met in the university library.

The Anesthesia of Addiction

When Max stopped anesthetizing himself with work and then with alcohol, he started to feel, and that was critical to finding himself.

Confronting your pain will not paralyze you. It will allow new parts of you to be born.

It is no different for those who use other pathological behaviors to anesthetize themselves. Compulsive gambling, sexual addictions, addiction to nicotine, and addiction to food are all behavioral ways that people avoid the pain that could ultimately be their path to new, healthier chapters of their lives. And what's worse, far from insulating them from suffering, these strategies actually cause their suffering to skyrocket.

If you are hostage to any one of these behaviors, start thinking of it as a smoke screen that is covering up your pain and blocking your path to a better life.

If you are overweight, then losing weight is only the first reward you'll get from dieting. Finding your*self* is the greater reward.

If you are a compulsive gambler, keeping your money is only the first way you enrich yourself by staying away from the track. Finding yourself is the greater way.

If you are spending your time and energy and risking your health as a slave to a sexual addiction, protecting yourself is only the first benefit of self-control. Finding yourself is the greater benefit.

If you are smoking to save yourself from feelings of depression or anxiety, saving yourself from cancer at age fifty or sixty or seventy is only one stunning benefit of stopping. Finding yourself is another.

The path to being a more complete and effective and loving person is *through* pain. Try to get around it, and you just lose yourself in it.

REPRESSED EMOTIONAL PAIN AND
PSYCHIATRIC DISTURBANCES

When we refuse to accept pain, it loses its meaning in the context of our life stories. It floats free from our capacity to understand it and becomes larger than life, intensifying and changing form. Denial fuels anxiety and insomnia and inattentiveness, but it also sets the stage for major depression, ADHD, anorexia and bulimia, post-traumatic stress disorder (PTSD), bipolar disorder, panic disorder, and even psychosis.

PTSD may be the best example. I have treated more than a hundred combat veterans hospitalized with the condition. Despite their determined efforts to avoid thinking about what they had lived through, and to stay away from anything (e.g., movies about war) that might remind them of it, they were haunted by "intrusive" memories and nightmares. Their buried pain resurrected itself with a vengeance. But many of these same veterans suffered other conditions, too, including profound major depression and panic disorder classified as "service connected." That means that the government believed those conditions had also resulted directly from their experiences as soldiers. Their denied suffering not only had burst through the mind's attempts to contain it (hence the flashbacks typical of PTSD) but had been transmuted into other very severe symptoms.

If denial fuels PTSD (and other psychiatric disorders), can confronting reality actually cure it? Indeed, it can. Many studies support the effectiveness of helping patients with PTSD to stop running from the traumas they have lived through.

Research on the use of Narrative Exposure Therapy (NET) helps prove the point. In NET, PTSD patients who have survived war or earthquakes or watching loved ones die or other traumas are encouraged to speak about or write about their life stories, starting in childhood and continuing right through vivid, moment-by-moment recollections of the extreme, sometimes catastrophic, events they have witnessed. And confronting these traumas significantly reduces their symptoms.

Think about that: simply confronting past trauma takes away the pathological power of that trauma.

Burying the past causes psychiatric disturbances. Resurrecting the past relieves those disturbances. *To the extent that a person accepts and shares the story of his or her suffering, that person frees himself or herself of it.*

In one pilot study (Onyut, Lamaro P., et al. 2005. Narrative Exposure Therapy as a treatment for child war survivors with post-traumatic stress disorder: Two case reports and a pilot study in an African refugee settlement. *BMC Psychiatry* 5:7), NET was used to help six children with PTSD who had arrived at a refugee settlement from Somalia, a country decimated by famine and war. At the beginning of treatment, the children remembered little of their earliest years or the particular traumas they had lived through. But they were able to recall much more after being gently and persistently encouraged to do so.

One child in the above study, who initially recalled very little of his childhood in Somalia, wrote:

> My mother had fair brown hair and skin. She was young and I loved her a lot. I was her firstborn and her favorite. She even told me so. My father was . . . hardworking. . . . Sometimes when he came home, he played with us in the evening. We played football together. . . .
>
> It was early in the morning. A group of about ten civilian men came to our house. They were armed with guns. . . .
>
> I stood very near to my parents. I was so scared. Suddenly I heard the sound of bullets. One of the [men] had started shooting. The moment I saw that he pulled

the trigger and heard the first bullet, I panicked. I started running. I felt such great fear. I ran inside the house and tried to hide. . . .

After a while I slowly moved toward the window and peeped out. What I saw was terrible. My mother and my father had been hit by the bullets. They were both lying on the ground. My mother had fallen on top of my father. . . . They had died.

This child had never really stopped running, because he had, over time, suppressed his memories and his emotional pain. And because he was unable to confront that suffering, it had taken on a life of its own in the form of classic symptoms of PTSD, such as terrifying flashbacks and intrusive memories of violence. Far from overpowering him with grief, NET helped him come out of hiding and master the darkness inside him by allowing him to "read," and thereby own, the darkest chapter of his life story.

The results of the study—including the change in this boy and the other children—were striking. While all six started the study with moderate to severe PTSD, by the end of it, four of the six children no longer met the criteria for PTSD. The remaining two had significantly reduced symptoms.

The healing path described in this book is, in some ways, like NET for those who have experienced toxic psychological stresses other than famine or war. It will help you resurrect the story of your suffering instead of just labeling the by-product of that suffering as OCD or PTSD or ADD or any other psychiatric disorder. It is, in a way, a safety "net," giving you a soft place to land when you peel away your shields, abandon your fictional histories, and fight your instincts to bury your pain. When you stop running from your suffering, you stop it from running your life. We heal by facing pain and feeling pain, never by fleeing pain.

Purging the Pain of the Past

A patient of mine named Nadine is a perfect example of someone who needed to face her past in order to heal. She was twenty-seven years old, five feet, four inches tall, and ninety pounds when she first came to see me. Her prior psychiatrist had moved out of state.

Since her teenage years, Nadine had stayed slim by making herself vomit after eating, a symptom of bulimia widely known as purging. But for about two years, she had also dramatically restricted her caloric intake, experienced almost no appetite (anorexia), and found her weight plummeting. She had become dehydrated again and again, requiring IVs to keep her electrolytes balanced and her blood pressure from bottoming out. Her tenuous medical status had made her quit her job and move back home with her mother and father.

Nadine didn't arrive at my office alone: she came with her parents. They had devoted themselves to helping her overcome her eating disorder from the time it became obvious—when she left for college at eighteen. Now they monitored everything she ate. They kept a chart of her daily weights. They gave her Zoloft and Xanax. They made certain she kept her doctors' appointments. They even listened outside the bathroom whenever she used it after a meal, to discourage her from purging. More than once, her father had to jimmy the bathroom door and physically restrain her to prevent her from making herself vomit.

When I greeted Nadine and her parents in the waiting area, she was seated between them, looking so slight as to be nearly invisible.

Nadine's father immediately stood up and shook my hand. Her mother did the same. Nadine stayed seated. The way she glanced at me, then resisted any further eye contact, reminded me of the way some of the adolescents I had treated initially checked me out.

I intentionally held back from saying whether Nadine's parents should join us for any part of our meeting together. I wanted to see whether they would suggest I take time with her alone before getting additional history from them. But the reverse happened. Her father asked whether he and his wife could spend a few minutes alone with me before *Nadine* joined us.

It wasn't hard to see that Nadine was behaving and being treated like a child. I decided to make it plain that I wasn't going to treat her that way. "It's up to Nadine," I said. "It's her appointment."

Nadine glanced at me again, a slight glimmer in her eye, then shrugged and looked away.

Her mother couldn't take my hint. "Why don't we just take a few minutes of your—" she started.

If Nadine wasn't going to take any control back from her parents, I decided the next best thing was for her to watch me do it. "Let's see if that makes sense *after* I talk to Nadine," I said.

Her parents reluctantly sat back down.

Nadine followed me to my office. For our first few minutes together, she made no eye contact, twirling her hair nervously while she checked out the art on my walls.

I decided not to start a struggle with her by asking her questions designed to "make" her talk to me. I wanted her to know I meant what I said to her parents. It was *her* appointment. She could do as much or as little with it as she wanted.

"They don't know when to back off," she said finally. "But they're just doing what they think is best for me."

Nadine sounded as if she were parroting what her parents might have told her when she was five or six or seven and being punished for bad behavior. *We're just doing what's best for you.*

"Are you certain they *know* what's best for you?" I asked.

"They have no idea," she said. "They spend all this time trying to get me to eat, which is ridiculous. I eat when I need to."

That was clearly untrue, as evidenced by the fact that Nadine's medical records included blood tests showing abnormal electro-lyte levels and EKGs with dangerous heart arrhythmias. Her assertion was another invitation for me to struggle with her, mimicking the tug-of-war she was engaged in with her parents and her internist and her nutritionist. I didn't take her up on it. "I'm not interested in your eating," I said.

"Oh, really?" she asked doubtfully. "What are you interested in?"

"Everything else."

"Such as . . ."

"Such as how and why you've gotten your parents to treat you like you're a child."

She smiled. "It comes naturally to them." She paused. "Three weeks from now, they'll be my legal guardians. They're going to court to have me declared incompetent."

That was something I hadn't been told by Nadine's parents. And it was a dramatic example of Nadine's regression to a child-like state. Soon, in the eyes of the law, she *would be* a child. "Will you fight it?" I asked her.

"Why fight?" she replied. "It'll make things easier. This way, if they want me to have a feeding tube, they can have me admitted to a hospital and force-fed."

"So you won't have to decide whether to eat anymore," I said. "They'll just decide for you."

"It's simpler."

A feeding tube is a rubber tube surgically inserted through the abdominal wall. Liquefied food (including nutritional supplements) can then be "pushed" through the tube directly into the stomach. The fact that Nadine saw her tug-of-war with her parents leading to that kind of intrusion on her autonomy was graphic evidence of how intense her struggle with them had become and how she expected it to end—in defeat. But it also felt as if it might be a metaphor for past trauma. After all, Nadine's body would be penetrated, and she would be passively "accepting" the violation (after having been officially defined as a child by the courts).

If Nadine's psychiatric disorders and their treatment were metaphors for the painful chapters of her life story, the four themes of those chapters would include resisting things entering her body; purging to get rid of what did enter her; struggling with others over the intrusion; and giving up and just letting it happen.

It's hard to miss how perfectly those themes reflect the drama of sexual abuse.

"I don't think having all your rights taken away from you and being force-fed is easy at all," I told her. "I think it's dehumanizing and terrifying."

Nadine looked at me in a way that seemed much more genuine, without her previous veneer of boredom or bitterness.

I went further out on a limb. "I wonder whether the reason you don't feel dehumanized or terrified," I said, "is that you've felt those things at some other time in your life and decided you were powerless to stop them."

"So you think you already know my whole story," she said.

I didn't think I knew Nadine's whole story, and I hadn't said that I did. Again, Nadine was asking to struggle with me—this time about how much of her truth I had intuited. And I didn't want her to waste any more of her energy struggling.

"I don't know your whole story," I said. "Not even close. It would take time before you could trust me and trust yourself enough to talk about what you've lived through instead of what you eat or don't eat. Maybe you'll never talk to me about it. But I'm here to help you whenever you want the help . . . on one condition."

"There's always a catch," she said, seemingly still intent on engaging me in a tug-of-war. "Tell me the rules. It's your office."

"It's my office, but it's your life," I said, "so the rules are simple: If you decide you want to work together, you have to call and book the appointment yourself. You have to come here by yourself. And you have to pay for the sessions yourself, even if that means I have to charge next to nothing at the beginning. Later on, if we can get you back to work, you'll pay full freight."

She smiled a more honest and relaxed smile. It was a smile that acknowledged we were talking about getting to the heart of something *meaningful* together, not agreeing to distract each other with power plays. Whenever a person becomes convinced that another human being is committed to listening to his or her real story, an instant and genuine interpersonal bond is possible. The foundation for empathy is built.

She laughed. "What if I don't like your rates?" she asked.

"Then you tell me to take a hike."

"I have to tell you all my secrets?"

"You don't *have* to tell me anything."

She studied me for a few seconds. "I guess I'll give it a try," she said. "At least while it's free."

Five minutes later, I walked Nadine back to the lobby.

Her father and mother stood up immediately.

"That was quick," her dad said, looking as though he expected a report from me on the spot. "What's your take?"

"Not out here, honey," Nadine's mother said to him. She looked at me. "Did you want all of us now, or should Nadine wait out here?" she asked.

I now had an opportunity to demonstrate that I really meant what I told Nadine in my office: this was her therapy, and hers alone. "I don't think we need to meet right now," I told her mother. "Nadine and I decided that we'll meet one-on-one, whenever she wants to make her next appointment—if she chooses to."

"I'm not sure I understand," her father said.

Out of the corner of my eye, I saw Nadine watching me intently. I wanted to show her that her father could be resisted by a competent adult—something she could become, too. "Which part do you not understand?" I asked her father. "The part about my not needing to meet with the two of you, or the part about meeting with Nadine privately in the future?"

Her father seemed too angry to respond.

"I guess we just had it in mind," her mother said, "that we'd be involved."

"Not a great idea," I said. "This has to be Nadine's time. She has to want to be here for her own reasons. You can't force-feed anyone psychotherapy. It doesn't work."

Nadine's mom nodded and glanced nervously at her husband.

"We'll see how it goes," he said, rolling his eyes. "It's certainly not what we expected." He held his hand out for me to shake.

I took it.

"Good luck," he said with a chuckle. "You'll need it."

While Nadine's dad's sarcasm didn't help the therapeutic process, it was a tribute to him that he didn't short-circuit the process entirely, which he probably could have done. Deep down, I believe he wanted the truth to come out, too.

It took Nadine more than a week to call me for her next appointment. Maybe she was trying to find out if I would violate the terms of our deal and try to persuade her to come back. Maybe when I kept my distance she was satisfied she really could trust me. Because from that second meeting on, she began revealing herself, slowly at first, then at a faster and faster pace, as though the dam holding back her truth had started to leak, then given way completely. Within three weeks, she seemed committed to studying every page of the life story she had kept sealed for so long.

The heart of Nadine's story revolved around her older brother Patrick. When Nadine was ten and Patrick was fifteen, he began touching her sexually. It was tremendously confusing to Nadine: on the one hand she knew that what she was doing with her brother was "wrong" and needed to be kept secret (as he warned her); on the other hand she liked the attention her brother paid her and liked some of the physical sensations she experienced when he touched her. The touching—and Nadine's struggle with her own feelings—went on for more than two years. That meant that during a critical development stage, Nadine was truly involved in a tug-of-war with her own feelings—wanting and not wanting something, passively allowing her brother to "satisfy" her emerging needs for physical excitement and then feeling guilty about letting him do it.

It isn't a stretch to think of Nadine's battle with food as paralleling those conflicted sexual feelings—her oscillating between starvation and having her fill, then feeling guilty and purging. And it isn't hard to imagine that her parents would be coaxed to join the battle, partly because it is hard to see the scope of it as it begins and partly because it turns out they were intent on *not* seeing.

When Nadine was eleven, her father had walked into her brother's room while he was fondling her. Her father had pulled her out of his room, then gone back and screamed at her brother that he would be sent away if anything like that ever happened again. But nothing was done to monitor the situation. In fact, according to Nadine, it seemed that her parents were careful *not* to look for, or even stumble upon, evidence that the abuse was continuing.

Nadine's brother stopped abusing her for a few months, then started again, becoming more and more brazen as time went on, even using his fingers to penetrate her.

"How did you feel during the months your brother kept his distance?" I asked Nadine.

She shrugged.

I was careful not to show any emotion, not wanting to influence her response in any way.

"It's fucked up," she said.

I stayed silent, waiting.

She took a deep breath, let it out, then looked at me as timidly as any ten-year-old girl possibly could. "Part of me was relieved," she said. "Part of me missed it."

There was the truth, the tug-of-war in its starkest form, the struggle between appetite and disgust. These were the roots of the moment that was approaching, when Nadine would cede all her rights and all control to her parents, revert to the status of a child, and "just let it happen." In some terrible way, she might even have found yielding to her parents' decision to force-feed her oddly exciting, or at least strangely comforting. Because the dynamic unfolding in her hospital room would be at least a little bit like the one that had unfolded in her brother's bedroom.

As it turned out, that force-feeding never happened. Neither did an appearance in court. Because when I presented my thoughts to Nadine's parents, they struggled with them only for a little while, then accepted the fact that these explanations seemed to be in line with what was happening to their daughter. They agreed to drop their guardianship petition and to completely drop out of monitoring Nadine's weight, giving those responsibilities to a nurse skilled in treating patients with eating disorders. They left the stage of the drama upon which they and Nadine were playing out her childhood pain in metaphor and supported the need for Nadine to address her childhood pain in reality.

When Nadine's parents surrendered control and listened to what had happened under their roof, they demonstrated something much more powerful than all the efforts they had made to keep Nadine's weight normal. They showed that they loved her enough to face the truth, however threatening, however unsettling, however painful. They agreed to partner with her in unearthing her buried treasure—the conflicted, tortuous emotions with which she had been silently struggling for more than a decade.

Over the course of the next several months, as Nadine expressed more of her feelings about her older brother preying upon her, she slowly gained weight. It was as though opening the dark chapters of her life story had made her life real to her and much too valuable to trade for a tug-of-war over whether she would live at all.

Psychiatric disturbances, including PTSD, anorexia and bulimia, panic disorder, bipolar disorder, ADD, and OCD may be partially encoded in our genes or due to malfunctions of chemistry (which is why some medications help). But I believe they are always manifestations of dis-ease with one's life story. They are fueled by denial and relieved in large part by digging deep and finding the source of one's suffering.

If you or a loved one is struggling with any one of the conditions I have mentioned (or any other psychiatric disorder) and being treated with medication alone, don't settle for that kind of incomplete care. Get to the bottom of your symptoms using this book and find a psychiatrist dedicated to helping you uncover the truth, not merely to keeping you in check chemically.

WHICH FACE OF PAIN DO YOU WEAR?

Did you identify with any of the people profiled in this chapter? Did you recognize your own face of pain in any of their stories? Perhaps you saw yourself in Mary, who married an extremely controlling man and, after he died, began several relationships (personal and professional) with people who took advantage of her. Maybe you, like Naomi, have physical pain that neither you nor your doctor can explain. Or are you more like Max, who used alcohol as a shield to hide the guilt he felt over his father's life choices? It might be that Nadine's story of early sexual abuse and the resultant psychiatric disorder resonated with you.

My face(s) of pain is/are:
(*Examples:* "*My face of pain is* unexplained physical illness. I get headaches almost every day, and my doctor cannot find a cause." "*My face of pain is* interpersonal conflict. I'm always hooking up with controlling men who don't care about my needs.")

1. _____

_____

_____

2. _____

_____

_____

3. _____

_____

_____

4. _____

_____

_____

The first step in removing a face of pain is recognizing that it exists. The fact that you or someone you love is struggling with a psychiatric disorder such as depression, with serious relationship issues such as repeated divorces, with pathological behaviors such as alcoholism, or even with a physical illness such as hypertension is only part of the story. The whole story also includes the roots of repressed pain entwined with that suffering. And the only way to truly heal is to trace those roots back and confront the original psychological injuries that now manifest themselves in one of the four faces of pain.

In the next section of this book, you will begin to link your past to your present, starting with the early chapters of your life story.

PART TWO
HOW YOU GOT HERE

CHAPTER 5

Why We Deny the Truth

How does it happen that by the time we are adults, we live lives partly based on denial, fiction, and repression, depriving ourselves of the enormous personal power that comes from living the truth? Part of the answer is that as vulnerable children and adolescents, we began quietly recording our life stories— mentally writing autobiographies designed to make us feel safe and loved and to insulate us from the real psychological toll of thinking we were in any way at risk.

To do this, we had to see our parents, the people we relied on for our very survival, as being good or making good sense—even if they weren't or didn't, and even if it meant burying reality *and parts of our true selves* in service to a reassuring vision of our early life experiences.

Research data supports this tendency to window-dress. Some abused children selectively remember the rare *positive* experiences they had with those who abused them. Severely traumatized children may forget being abused altogether. And a child rejected by his or her father or mother will often identify with the *rejecting* parent in order to regain that parent's love, despite the fact that doing so means denying deeply held feelings of anxiety, shame, and anger.

Our truth was distorted not only by denying the hurts we suffered but by a kind of permeability to the narrative force of others. The way our parents, older siblings, teachers, and other caretakers interpreted (or spun) the meaning of the events unfolding around us influenced the way we came to understand them. We echoed and mimicked their perspectives because we wanted to rely on them and participate in a shared experience with them, and because we were still learning about ourselves and the world.

It is hard to imagine a five-year-old boy with an ability to see to the core of complex relationships. But even if he could, it would be difficult for him to resist the urgings of the adults around him to see those relationships differently. To do so would likely make the child feel too isolated, afraid, or guilty.

In other words, kids will surrender their version of reality to that of the powerful adults around them.

When the boy, for example, is unconsciously aware that his narcissistic mother is more dedicated to her own well-being than to his, he is likely to try to ally with her *around her needs,* abandoning his own, possibly even feeling guilty about them. The exaggerated bond he forms with his mother may later be interpreted as love, when it is really based in fear and a denial of self. And unless he digs down to the truth as an adult, he is likely to partner with another woman who exacts the same level of self-betrayal from him. Because it will feel like home.

When a little ten-year-old girl is unconsciously aware that her parents have love for her but not for each other, she may give up her own development to serve as the glue holding together their shaky union. The dissolution of her family becomes the monster she must keep at bay. She may choose to stay at home rather than go away to summer camp, or commute to college rather than live there, all in the interest of maintaining the fiction that her home life is secure. She might suffer panic disorder or depression that incapacitates her and legitimizes her having to stay at home long into adulthood. And unless and until she digs down to the truth that her parents have no real marriage and have been consciously or unconsciously using her to avoid that reality, she will be a slave to their lie. Even if she leaves home, it may be for a man who uses their union as camouflage for deep personal problems of his own. Because it will feel like home.

Without a real effort to see the dramas we lived through for what they were, not what we wished them to be, we will always find those dramas compelling.

The trouble is that, inside, many of us feel as vulnerable as we did when we were five or ten or twelve years old and are loath to start digging for the truth. And that prevents us from growing beyond the roles assigned to us in our families of origin and re-claiming our core authenticity—and the personal power that flows from it. It prevents us from living the truth.

THE DESIRE TO BE LOVED

Nothing in the human psyche is more powerful than the desire to be loved. And at no time is that desire stronger than in child-hood.

One of my patients, a thirty-seven-year-old single woman named Maggie, is a good example. She came to see me after los-ing her job as an executive at a clothing company barely a year after being hired. She'd never been fired before and said she felt "humiliated." The stress of starting a job search with a black mark on her résumé, she said, was keeping her up at night and preventing her from concentrating during the day. Her migraines, which she hadn't had since she was a teenager, were back.

"It would be one thing if I'd hated this woman from day

one," Maggie said of her boss, Elizabeth. "But I liked her. I trusted her. And she totally used me." She paused. "I thought I knew people. I was really stupid."

Maggie looked genuinely hurt. "How did she 'use' you?" I asked.

"I left a really, really good job at my last company because she recruited me. She was always telling me at trade shows how talented I was and how she'd love to work with me. Then she made me an offer. I took it. I poured my whole heart into her company. I definitely put in more time than I ever had before—eighty, ninety hours a week, traveling to Europe and China and everywhere else. It was nonstop for thirteen months. And then all of a sudden she's like, 'This isn't working out.' "

"Did she say why?"

"Ridiculous stuff," Maggie said. "My attitude. Shipping glitches, which I had zero control over." She paused. "From what I hear, this is just Elizabeth's thing. It happened to two other people who had the job before me. One lasted a year; the other, a year and a half. She gets nervous someone will take over or something."

"When did you find out about these other people?" I asked.

"People at the company told me before I signed on," she said. "I just thought it would be different with me."

"Why?"

"She said they acted like landing the job meant they didn't have to be hands-on anymore—like they could just sit back and delegate. And I pride myself on never asking anyone who works under me to do more than I do. Plus, I had this connection with her. Or I thought I did."

"What sort of connection was that?" I asked.

"She seemed to want to help me get to the next level," Maggie said. "I've never worked directly for a woman before. I've always thought it would be the best situation for me." She sighed. "Dumb."

"Not dumb," I assured her. "You wanted a mentor."

She shrugged. "I've just never felt completely comfortable with the men I've worked for. Maybe it's the glass-ceiling thing. Or maybe it's me. I don't know. It's been hard for me to trust men."

"Why is that?"

"Because my dad was an asshole."

That sounded pretty straightforward. "How so?"

"The usual way," she said. "He screwed around on my mother."

"Did they divorce?"

"When I was eleven. But that was after putting my mother through hell for years."

"You knew about your dad's infidelity?" I asked.

"My mother and I don't keep secrets from each other."

"She told you?"

"I found out about it the minute she did. I remember her screaming at him that he couldn't come to my seventh birthday party because she'd found a girl's number in his pocket." She smiled. "Sandra."

"Why are you smiling?" I asked.

She shrugged. "I just think it's funny I never forgot her name. The others are a blur."

The fact that Maggie had never forgotten the name of her father's first known lover isn't funny at all, of course. "You're not angry about what happened?" I asked

Her smile disappeared. "At him, nobody else. I hardly speak to him."

That made sense. At that age, Maggie would have been attached to her father in complex ways, including (at least according to Sigmund Freud) unconscious fantasies about becoming the sole focus of her father's affections, in place of her mother. The fact that she had had to acknowledge, at the age of seven, that her father was apparently passionate about a third woman—a stranger—would have made her feel jealous and enraged.

But Maggie's words told me more than that. She seemed intent on my hearing that she was angry at "only" her father. And that *didn't* make sense to me. It felt as if she were constructing a barrier to keep herself—and me—from the truth. After all, two people had hurt Maggie: Her father had done it by being careless and callous enough to disclose his sexual indiscretions. Her mother had done it by sharing highly charged information with Maggie when the little girl was clearly incapable of understanding it. From the moment Maggie's mother learned of her husband's infidelity, she had apparently used Maggie as a pawn to get back at him, barring him from showing up at their daughter's seventh birthday party.

But Maggie couldn't have allowed herself to feel angry at both her parents. That would have made her feel too alone. Knowing that her father could leave for another woman, she would have needed to believe that someone would protect and love her forever. She turned to her mother, even though it didn't sound to me like her mother had earned her confidence.

"You're very close with your mom?" I asked.

"She's my best friend," Maggie said. "We've been through everything together."

It turned out, in fact, that Maggie had signed on with her mother for war after war. There were her father's repeated infidelities. There was her parents' divorce. Then there were the half dozen or so tumultuous romances her mother suffered through, each of them ending with the discovery that her boyfriend was either married or addicted to drugs or seeing other women.

In turn, Maggie's mom had come to her daughter's defense each time Maggie chose a man "unworthy" of her trust or affection. And that happened a lot. Even at work, her male bosses always seemed to be egotists, predators, or frauds. And her mother was always there, a shoulder to cry on.

I knew that challenging Maggie's belief that her mother was beyond reproach would connect her with early and intense feelings of fear and betrayal. I would be asking her to feel all the pain she would have felt at seven had she admitted to herself that neither her father nor her mother was able to put her first, that she wasn't *that* well-loved by anyone. To a child, that would have felt like the whole world could fall apart at any time, that her very survival was in question. And part of Maggie was still that child.

I also knew, though, that Maggie had come to therapy after her *female* employer disappointed her. And she had come to *me*—a man—for help. That told me she might be ready to abandon the gender stereotypes and family myths that were keeping her from seeing the true nature of her predicament as a child—and moving beyond it.

"Why wasn't your mother more careful to keep what she found out about your father to herself?" I asked Maggie during our next session.

She squinted at me in disbelief. "You're joking, right?"

"Not at all."

She stood up. "This is ridiculous. How can you be taking his side?"

"I'm not," I said. "I'm taking yours."

She started toward the door.

I wanted to make sure Maggie understood that I believed her leaving would be a form of denial. "You can't avoid the truth forever," I said.

She turned back to me. "It was her job to cover for him?" she seethed.

"That's not what I'm saying," I said gently. I motioned toward Maggie's seat, hoping she'd take it again.

She didn't move.

"It was her job to protect your relationship with him, even after he violated theirs," I said.

"There was nothing to protect."

"Maybe not," I allowed. I paused. "Do you remember anything about your dad from when you were, say, five or six?"

"Nothing good," she said.

I nodded but stayed silent. Several seconds passed.

"What are you getting at?" Maggie asked. "I mean, he took me to the park and stuff. What father doesn't? But when it came to—"

Plenty of fathers don't. "What sort of park?" I asked.

"A *park*. I don't know. It wasn't anything special. It had this really high slide and swings and rides, or whatever."

"What did you like to do there?"

That was a simple question, but it opened up memories that Maggie had shut down in order to maintain a version of her life story that was partly fiction: that her father was the enemy and her mother was her only ally.

She rolled her eyes. "I don't know why this matters."

"Tell me anyhow."

She sighed. "The slide, okay? You went up a ladder that must have had about twenty steps and . . ." She stopped herself. "What does this have to do with . . . ?"

I thought of my own daughter, six years old at the time. I could picture her at the top of a slide like the one Maggie had described, half excited, half petrified. "Did he tell you you'd be all right sliding down?" I asked Maggie. "Did he wait for you at the bottom?"

She just looked at me. Her eyes filled with tears. She wiped them, then shook her head. "Why are you doing this?"

I pressed forward. "What else did you two do together?"

A tear rolled down Maggie's cheek. "He drove me to school every day."

"Did you like that?"

Another tear. "Stop," Maggie said. She finally sat down.

I did stop, but her tears didn't—for half a minute, maybe more.

During our next meeting, I pressed Maggie to remember more of the good times she had had with her father. I also started helping her more realistically evaluate her mother's behavior. "Did you think your mom had bad luck choosing men?" I asked. "Or bad judgment?"

"How was she supposed to know if some guy was a loser?"

"Guy after guy?"

"She's supposed to be a mind reader?"

"No, just a mother. And that means being careful who she includes in her daughter's life."

Maggie looked me straight in the eye, as if deciding whether she could really trust me. "I guess I would have been more careful if I were her," she said finally, just above a whisper.

It didn't take more than a few hours for Maggie to make the connection between her mother having selected one damaged man after another and her own habit of doing the same. Not only was she deprived of the love of her father from a young age but she never learned how to include a worthy man in her life.

I remembered Maggie telling me her reasoning for thinking that a female employer would be the right fit for her. *I've just never felt completely comfortable with the men I've worked for.*

Is that any wonder? Having seen her father unmasked as a philanderer and then portrayed as a pure scoundrel, then having witnessed the predictable results of her mother continuing to favor broken, unreliable men, Maggie had almost no chance of drawing any conclusion other than that *all* men were untrustworthy, even her male employers. Why would she have ever looked to one of them for nurturance or mentoring?

Remember the words of Carl Jung: "That which we do not bring to consciousness appears in our lives as fate."

I didn't even have to ask Maggie the question most directly related to her having misjudged the character of the woman who hired her away from her prior job, encouraged her to work ninety hours a week, then summarily fired her, apparently for no good reason. Maggie asked that question herself. "You know, I never even considered believing that Elizabeth had fired two other people for no reason. Do you think," she wondered aloud, "that wanting to see my mother as perfect meant I couldn't really see Elizabeth for who she was?"

The key word there was "couldn't." Maggie couldn't let herself see the truth about Elizabeth because it was linked to core truths she was denying about her mother. "It feels to me like you wanted very badly to believe a woman would protect and nurture you, because that's what you wanted to believe as a little girl."

The unconscious life-story link between Maggie's childhood and adulthood was the reason her being fired had kept her up at night, rekindled her migraines, stolen her concentration, and made her feel humiliated. It was also the reason she had come to therapy. The link between *now* and *then* had brought her uncomfortably close to a truth that would have been much too threatening for her to accept as a child: that a woman who seemed to care about her and have her best interests at heart was actually putting her own needs first.

Now, as an adult, Maggie could finally afford to see that truth, to feel it, and to stop limiting herself by trying to avoid it. The reality that would have felt as if it were the end of the world at age seven, that—back then—could have driven her into an unremitting, deep depression or a constant state of panic, was still terribly sad but bearable at thirty-seven.

She stopped thinking of her mother as her only friend and beyond reproach and began seeing her as a complex person with both strengths and weaknesses. And while that caused a temporary rift in their relationship, it also made their bond real and laid the foundation for growth in even more honest directions in the future.

Maggie's next position was as a vice president at a clothing company, with a man at the helm. But unlike her routine with every other man she had worked for, she checked his reputation for integrity extensively before signing on. She told him she was looking for more than a job—that she wanted a mentor. She guarded against her predictable tendency (rooted in her childhood experiences) to write him off as duplicitous, insincere, or arrogant. And she found what she would have sworn didn't exist in the world: a man who actually ended up coming through for her.

Her luck in romance eventually changed, too. Knowing that she might unconsciously choose men with character flaws (because they were the kind of men she had watched her mother date), she intentionally slowed down her next few relationships until she could feel more certain she was with someone reliable—or she'd walk away. She actually avoided one man who was very handsome and had led a very exciting life (and had been married twice before) because, as she put it, "I'm mesmerized by trouble—at the beginning. Later on, it's a nightmare." And she met someone who initially bored her but eventually won her heart by being passionate yet trustworthy.

The stereotypes of her father and mother that Maggie had clung to like a life raft as a child had become an anchor weighing her down in adulthood. Now, having let go of them, far from drowning, she found herself free.

Being an adult with her own personal resources (money, access to friends, a skill set that provided real self-esteem) is just one reason Maggie was able to deal with realities she once feared would do her in. Another is that together we unearthed what felt to her like the *true story* of her pain—the loss of her relationship with her father and her clinging to an unreliable mother. And knowing the true source of one's pain makes it easier to bear.

Dimitrios Oreopoulos, MD, writing about physical pain in *Humane Medicine* (and echoing the work of Eric Cassell in his classic paper "The Nature of Suffering and the Goals of Medicine," published in the *New England Journal of Medicine*), put it this way: "Frequently, people in pain report suffering if the pain is overwhelming and they feel out of control, *if the source of pain and its meaning are unknown* [emphasis mine], or when they perceive the pain as a threat to their continued existence, not merely to their lives but to their integrity as persons."

Psychological pain is no different. Knowing its true source is the key to overcoming it.

We are all made up of stories. As children we turned those stories partly into fiction in order to survive psychologically and feel loved—to keep our pain at bay. But as adults, clinging to the fiction becomes the source of even greater suffering.

Your Own Desire to Be Loved

Think about the people who were most important to you during your childhood years, and answer the questions below.

In my story, as a child and as a young adult, who was there for me with unconditional love?

_____

_____

In my story, as a child and as a young adult, who did I feel put conditions on their love, and what were those conditions? (Examples: "My father loved me when I excelled at sports." "My sister loved me when I took the blame for her misdeeds.")

My _____ *loved me when I:*

_____

_____

_____

And that made me feel:
(*Example: "My sister loved me when I took the blame for her misdeeds, and that made me feel* that everything that went wrong was somehow my fault.")

_____

_____

_____

_____

The events or patterns of behavior displayed by my mother or father that were not *loving included:*
(*Example: "The events or patterns of behavior displayed by my mother or father that were* not *loving included* when my mother constantly asked me to take her side in arguments she had with my father. Or when my father told me I could be beautiful *if* I lost weight.")

_____

_____

_____

_____

If I were to write to my mother or father or a sibling (or someone else who was really important to me) about the way(s) in which his or her love was really hard to feel deep down, I would say:
(*Example:* "Dad, you're always saying how much you love me and how special I was to you growing up. But it's pretty hard to really *feel* that, considering the fact that you only visited every other weekend after you divorced mom. Mom says you had 'full visitation' and could have been around a lot more. Why weren't you? I think I've always sort of assumed that I was an embarrassment to you or an inconvenience.")

_____

_____

_____

_____

_____

_____

_____

_____

THE DESIRE TO FEEL SAFE

When we are young, we look up to our parents. We don't see them as human beings; we see them as our role models and our protectors. They are there to keep us loved and sheltered, physically and psychologically.

But parents are, after all, human and therefore flawed. And were they to fall off the pedestals on which we place them, they could crush our own tender psyches in the process. So, too often, we prop them up in our imaginations, denying who they really are and what we really lived through.

Tom, another patient of mine, helps prove this point. He was forty-four years old when he first came to see me. He felt stuck. He managed a car dealership and made a good living but hated his work.

"I've been with the same dealership fifteen years," he told me. He rubbed his tired-looking eyes. "I started selling cars there and got promoted to assistant manager, then manager. It's been the same routine since then, going on six years now. I get there at eight in the morning and leave at nine or ten at night, usually six days a week. And there isn't an hour when I don't feel like I'm wasting my life."

I knew from other patients of mine in the car business that salespeople and managers tended to move frequently from dealership to dealership. "It's unusual to be at one shop for fifteen years, isn't it?" I asked Tom.

"Basically unheard-of," he said. "Anyone else would be general manager of a group of dealerships by now."

"Why not you?" I asked.

"My dad always asks me the same question. I've had offers. But it never seemed like the right time. First it was that I was getting married and didn't want another big change in my life at the same time. Then it was having my son. Then my daughter." He sighed. "The truth is I'll always find some reason to stay put."

"Even though you hate it there . . ."

"I'm not sure it would be any different at another shop," he said. "I hate the work, not the place." He shook his head. "I pretty much hate myself at this point."

"Or maybe you just *aren't* yourself," I said. "Is there something you'd rather be doing with your life?"

"You mean, like a dream job?" He looked at me almost timidly, as if simply uttering the words filled him with anxiety.

I nodded.

"If I could do anything in the world, I'd open a restaurant. I've got a great idea for one. Honestly, I think that's what's kept me going the past ten years." He shook his head. "Not that I'd ever actually do it."

"Are you worried you wouldn't be good at it?"

Tom smiled. He suddenly looked much more energized. "I'm not worried about that. I'm a very good cook and a really good manager," he said. "Cooking's my only hobby. It's the only thing I read about. The only TV I watch is the Food Network." He paused. "I think I could be great."

I could tell from Tom's voice and his eyes that he meant what he was saying. "Is it the financial risk, then?" I asked.

"No," Tom said. "I'm a mess, not my finances. I've put away a little dough. And if I opened a place and it went belly-up, I could get a job managing another dealership in no time at all. My dad always tells me I should just go for it, but for some reason I can't pull the trigger."

That was the second time Tom had mentioned his father. "Sounds like your dad really believes in you," I said.

"He believes in himself," Tom said. "That's the difference between us. He has more courage in his little finger than I have in my whole body."

The fact that Tom had sidestepped my statement about his father believing in *him* told me to dig deeper into their relationship. "Tell me more about him," I said.

"He has courage," Tom said. "If he has a hunch, he follows it."

"Such as?"

"Google," Tom said.

"Google?"

"He mortgaged his house to invest in Google when it went public. It went to the moon. Now he's living large."

Tom's dad mortgaging his house to invest in the IPO of an

Internet stock sounded more impulsive to me than courageous. "Is that the first time he's laid everything on the line for what he believed in?" I asked.

"He's always been that way," Tom said with pride. "As long as I can remember."

When I dug deeper, though, it became clear that some of what Tom remembered about his dad wasn't anything to be proud of. When Tom was nine years old, his father invested almost everything the family owned in developing, patenting, and trying to market an invention designed to make cars more fuel efficient. When it turned out the technology didn't work well enough to interest any of the automakers, his father had to sell their home and move the family into his own parents' house for two years while he got back on his feet by working as an insurance agent. Six years later, he left that job to partner with friends in Texas who were convinced a large piece of land for sale there included vast deposits of gold. When none was found, he declared bankruptcy and told Tom he no longer had the money to pay for his college education. So Tom dropped out during his first semester and never went back.

"Were you very upset with him?" I asked Tom.

"Not for a second," Tom said without hesitation. "My father gave us all the courage we needed. He told us not to worry about a thing, that he'd make everything back, and more. And ultimately he did exactly what he said he would."

"With the Google investment?" I asked.

Tom nodded.

"That was a long time after your college years."

Tom chuckled. "He didn't say *when* he'd make it back."

Staying Safe (and Sorry)

Just as Maggie had used the word "funny" in reference to remembering the name of her father's lover, Tom was using humor to distance himself from the reality that his father had squandered the chance for him to go to college. And humor was only one of his defenses against that fact. His view of his father as a courageous man with complete confidence in himself shielded Tom from a realization that would have been utterly terrifying to him as a boy: that his father was a self-involved gambler with terrible judgment who was willing to risk his family's financial well-being, including their home and his child's education, to indulge his narcissistic fantasies of unlimited wealth.

It's one thing to go after your dreams. It's another to go off panning for gold and forget about your mortgage payment and your son's tuition bill.

Imagine a little boy packing his things and leaving his room, his house, and his neighborhood forever. There isn't much chance he would do anything but cling to his father for reassurance and construct an airtight image of him as brave and strong, *despite the fact that his father's very real weaknesses are, in effect, the source of the boy's suffering.*

Once I saw how Tom was fictionalizing his father, it was easy to understand why he had never pursued his own genuine dream of opening a restaurant. In his mind, following his heart was unconsciously connected with being just like his "courageous" dad—reckless, insensitive to the needs of his family, bankrupt, and homeless. He had "courage" all mixed up with "chaos" because he was still too afraid to dig down to the truth and see his father for who he really was.

"You know, I was thinking about something you told me," I said during our next session. "When you listed the reasons you hadn't switched dealerships and taken a job as a general manager, the first items on your list related to making sure your marriage and your children stayed secure."

"Excuses," Tom said.

"But good ones, as excuses go," I said. I wanted to challenge

Tom to think about his father in a more honest light. "You didn't want your kids to have to go through what you did with your own father."

"We ended up doing great."

"Really?" I said. "You hate your work, and you won't take the risk to do what you love."

"That has nothing to do with my father."

I kept pressing. "You're saying you wouldn't feel guilty if you lost your house and couldn't send your kids to college?"

"Of course I would. I mean . . ."

"Do you think your father felt guilty?"

"I don't know. I mean . . ."

"Did he tell you he did?"

"Well, no, but some things speak for—"

"Did you ever see him cry over it?"

Tom stayed silent.

"Sleepless nights? Anything?"

Tom looked away. "He was a tough guy," he said softly, as though barely clinging to his fiction.

"And you had to pretend to be one," I said, "at nine." I paused. "Where do you think all your fear went?"

"I guess I kept it."

"Exactly. But when you keep fear bottled up, denying it even exists, it takes more and more of your energy, until it paralyzes you completely." I waited a few moments, then made my point. "When your dad followed his dreams, other people got badly hurt, including you. But you're not nine anymore. You could pursue your dream without turning it into anyone else's nightmare. Worse comes to worst, the restaurant closes and you go back to work at a car dealership. You still keep your house and put your kids through school. You've earned that safety net by working sixteen-hour days for fifteen years. There's no shame in that."

"I guess not," Tom said, his voice suddenly less stressed. "I just never looked at it that way." We sat in silence for several moments.

"So now that you've got the safety net," I said, "it's time for a leap of faith. My guess: the safety net never gets used."

Tom opened his restaurant about a year later. And while there were moments he was certain he would fail, that he should retreat back to the car business before losing everything, he stayed the course. Because he understood most of his fear of chaos was coming from being powerless when he lost his home at nine years old, and when he lost his chance for a college education at seventeen.

His restaurant eventually began to thrive.

Your Own Desire to Be Safe

Once again, think about the people who were most important to you during your childhood years and answer the questions below in terms of your desire to be safe.

In my story, as a child and as a young adult, the person who made me feel safest was:
(*Example: "In my story, as a child and as a young adult, the person who made me feel safest was my older brother."*)

But being close to that person exposed me to some pain, too, including:
(*Example: "But being close to that person exposed me to some pain, too, including the fact that my older brother was ten years older than me, and I felt abandoned when he went away to college and left me at home with my verbally abusive father."*)

_____

_____

_____

_____

And that made me feel:
(*Example:* "*My brother abandoned me when he went away to college, and that made me feel* that men will let you down when you need them most.")

_____

_____

_____

_____

If _____ *had not been in my life as a child, I would have felt totally alone. But dealing with him/her certainly meant coping with:*
(*Example:* "*If* Uncle Fred *had not been in my life as a child, I would have felt totally alone. But dealing with him certainly meant coping with* the fact that he was a terrible alcoholic.")

_____

_____

_____

_____

The reason I always wince when my mother/father/sister/brother/ childhood friend talks about how great things were for us growing up is:
(*Example: "The reason I always wince when my mother/father/ sister/brother/childhood friend talks about how great things were for us growing up is* that it wasn't so great because we were so poor.")

_____

_____

_____

_____

The most anxiety-provoking part of my childhood was:
(*Example: "The most anxiety-provoking part of my childhood was* when my brother was diagnosed with leukemia, and my parents got very, very quiet about the whole thing. It made me sort of feel like I might get sick, too, and I remember constantly looking in the mirror to see if I was getting pale. But I also felt guilty for worrying about myself so much when my brother was the one with the illness.")

_____

_____

_____

_____

_____

Even though I had a pretty decent life growing up, I'd like to spare my own kids:
(*Example: "Even though I had a pretty decent life growing up, I'd like to spare my own kids* the constant moving around we did. I think it made it tough for me to form friendships back then. But I also think it makes me feel as if all friendships are temporary, even now. I sometimes think I end friendships over little arguments just because I'm always thinking they're about to end anyway.")

_____

_____

_____

_____

_____

Tom and Maggie are like many of us. Much of what stands in the way of our becoming the people we are meant to be in this world is fear from childhood and adolescence that we hold in our hearts and our heads and the pits of our stomachs. We think that unearthing it will be the end of us. But it never is. It is always a beginning.

Confronting the painful truths in our life stories might have been impossible when we were children who needed to believe, in order to function day to day, that we were safe and loved and that our worlds made sense. But as adults, facing those truths and living the lessons they teach can only free us. It has for me. It did for Maggie, and it did for Tom. It has for hundreds of patients I have had the privilege to know during my fifteen years in practice. And it will for you, too.

CHAPTER 6

Why We Repeat the Past

You would think that even though we deny our truths and run from the painful chapters of our life stories, we would at least learn from our "grown-up" experiences to stop making the same mistakes over and over again. We'd pick one inappropriate mate, and when that didn't work out, we'd make a better choice in the future. We'd take on so many ambitious projects at the same time, we couldn't possibly accomplish them all; we'd fail miserably and learn to be more judicious going forward. But as many of us know all too well, we don't seem to profit much from the errors of our ways. Our attempts to keep our pain buried will, in and of themselves, lead to our reexperiencing it, in one form or another, again and again.

Why? Because, like planets held in orbit by gravitational fields, human beings gravitate toward high-energy psychological dynamics—whether those dynamics are conscious or not. And buried pain is the most magnetic psychological force of all. Left to simmer underground, it becomes irresistible and draws us back into the destructive patterns of emotion and behavior that first created it.

To choose a graphic example, if you were terrified of your violent father as a little girl and resolve to run away from that reality, you will habitually run right back into trouble. You will either gravitate toward one violent man after another (because those men will reawaken your intense childhood desire to be loved by your father) or try to stay safe by selecting men who are incapable of expressing any anger (and need, for example, to use alcohol to quell their repressed emotions). In either case, the relationships will be rooted in unexplored, powerful childhood anxieties, and your suffering will be reborn as the main character in one painful drama after another.

Remember, you can't outdistance your past. The truth always wins.

I once went to a bachelor party and ended up talking to the naked dancer. I asked her if she liked her work.

"I love it," she said. "The first time I got up on stage, I felt completely at home."

"What was home like?" I asked.

That was enough to make her eyes fill with tears.

Nothing can compete energetically with the demons we have stored away since childhood; we remember them, after all, with a child's heart and mind.

An appearance of mine on *The Oprah Winfrey Show* focused on women whose fathers had sexually abused them. These women went on to marry men who ended up sexually abusing the children they had together.

"How could these women allow that to happen?" the audience wondered. "Knowing the pain they themselves had been through, how could they not intuit that they were exposing their children to similar traumas? How could they not *see* what was happening?"

The answer is that the women on the show had not fully confronted their pain. They had not looked plainly at the special hell it was to love their fathers while being manipulated and assaulted by them. The complexity of that dynamic—being victimized and still wanting the warm embrace of their victimizers—was the most mind-bending, horrific part of what they had been through. By not examining it in detail and extinguishing its *magnetic* energy, they were still attracted to it and fell "in love" with other manipulative, assaultive men.

THE MAGNETIC FORCE OF PSYCHOLOGICAL PAIN

The story of one of my own patients, a thirty-nine-year-old woman named Paula, proves that people can orbit the same buried pain again and again.

Paula finally faced her own demons when her third marriage ended, like the prior two, in disaster. When she first came to see me, she was trying to cope with the suicide of her third husband, which had left her nine-year-old daughter fatherless. She felt terribly sad but also extremely guilty.

"I should have done something," she said through tears. "He told me once a few months ago that he didn't want to live. I just never believed he'd actually do something crazy."

I have spoken with dozens of family members over the years who have lost loved ones to suicide. I always reassure them, as I did Paula, that those closest to a depressed person are often in the worst position to rationally evaluate how dangerous the situation really is. They may want to believe that their love and support will be enough to sustain the person. They may be too afraid to face the thought of losing the person. They may be angry at the notion that the person could actually choose death over life with them. Or they may, like so many people, be laboring under the false belief that those who talk about ending their own lives never do (a dangerous myth). When I shared these facts with Paula, however, she remained inconsolable.

"I can't help feeling I'm somehow responsible," she said. "I mean, he was fine when I married him."

"Depression strikes all kinds of people," I said. "It isn't something you would have been able to predict."

She shook her head. "This isn't the first time a man has fallen apart around me," she said. She paused. "It happened to my other husbands, too."

It turned out that each of Paula's first two marriages had ended when her husband fell victim to a debilitating mental illness. In the first case, it was alcoholism. In the second, it was depression and addiction to narcotic pain relievers. And each man ultimately left *her*, not the other way around.

Wondering whether Paula was reproducing a dynamic she had witnessed in her parents' marriage, I asked her to tell me about them.

"They're still together," she said. "Forty-five years. They still hold hands. To this day, my father says my mom's his 'little guardian angel.' He still calls me his 'princess.' It's like I grew up in a fairy tale."

I have learned by now that when people tell you straight out that their lives are make-believe, you should believe them.

I went looking for the part of Paula's life that was fiction. "Did your father need a guardian angel?" I asked.

"What do you mean?"

"Did he need your mother to take care of him or protect him?" I asked.

She shook her head. "Not even close," she said. "He's the exact opposite of the men I married."

"In what way is he different?" I asked.

"He's just . . . *commanding*," she said. "He was captain of his college football team, a captain in the army, head of a law firm. He's a take-charge person. I don't think he's *ever* fallen apart."

"Did he take charge of your mother?" I asked.

"Without a doubt. She pretty much lives for him," Paula said.

"More than for you?"

Paula fell silent for a while. "My father always took up a lot of space in a room," she said.

The truth was that Paula's father hadn't given anyone enough room to breathe. He had insisted on a regimented home life. He expected his "little guardian angel" wife to serve dinner at the same time each evening, to keep the house white-glove clean, and to make sure Paula and her older brother did not disturb him as he worked at home late into the night. He expected Paula and her brother to meet his standards in terms of their academic performance, the appropriateness and neatness of their dress, their commitment to athletics, their choice of friends, even what they ate.

That didn't sound exactly like an "ideal marriage" or "fairy tale" home life.

"It seems like you, your mom, and your brother spent a lot of time satisfying him," I said.

"I've honestly never thought of it that way," she said. "I never considered *not* satisfying him. None of us did."

Whether or not Paula thought much about it, having lived like a soldier, taking orders from her "commanding" father, she might not have been up for "reenlisting" with another powerful man. I wondered whether she had unconsciously chosen her husbands because she intuited they were broken in some way and in no position to exert control over her. "How did you meet your first husband?" I asked her.

"College," she said. "We dated all of junior and senior year. After graduation I went to work for a public relations company in New York, and he stayed in Boston to start law school. We really missed each other. He proposed within a few weeks."

"And then you moved to Boston?" I asked.

"No. He moved to New York four months later."

"He transferred to another law school?"

She shook her head. "Law school wasn't going well for him anyhow."

"Meaning?"

"He really missed me," she said. "I think he got a little depressed and started drinking. He ended up withdrawing from school and coming to New York. I got him a job as an assistant to one of the executives at the company where I was working."

The fact that Paula was downplaying such a significant event in her first husband's life—depression or alcoholism or both—made me wonder how accepting she was of him being the weak one in the relationship. "Was that the same sort of position you had at the company?" I asked.

"No," she said. "I was in the management training program. He was kind of like . . . well, a glorified secretary type, I guess."

That didn't sound very glorious—working at least a few rungs beneath your fiancée in a job that has nothing to do with your goals, after dropping out of law school. "Did he stop drinking?" I asked.

"For a little while. But then it got worse."

"Were you worried?"

She shrugged. "I always figured he was strong enough to beat it."

Paula's first husband wasn't strong enough to get sober, of course. He was weak and struggling. He had felt so alone that he popped the question within a few weeks of her moving to another city. He had missed her so much after their engagement that he started to drink and dropped out of law school. He had seemed happy enough to take the job she got him as a "glorified secretary" at the company where she was training to be an executive.

After his alcoholism accelerated, and after he lost his job at the public relations firm, and after he finally entered AA and started seeing a psychiatrist who treated his underlying depression, he left her. He told her his alcohol counselor believed she was enabling his illness and that his recovery required him to stand on his own two feet.

He was right. Paula had always been ready to catch him when he stumbled. Because whenever he did, it reminded her she was stronger than he was, that he needed her and that she was at no risk of being overwhelmed by a powerful man like her father.

Paula was introduced to her second husband by her brother, Ted, himself a former cocaine abuser. He introduced Paula to his sponsor in Narcotics Anonymous, a man sober from narcotic pain relievers (such as Percocet and OxyContin) for more than ten years.

"Your first husband was an alcoholic," I said to Paula. "Then you started dating someone who'd been addicted to drugs. Did you worry about that?"

"He'd beaten it," she said. "Isn't that a sign of strength?"

Beating an addiction requires great strength, but addiction and its psychological roots are very powerful, too. That's why addicts relapse so frequently. "How long did he stay sober after you got married?" I asked.

Paula took a deep breath, let it out. "A little more than eight months," she said. "I did everything I could to help him. When he started using again, I even told him he should just leave his job and focus on getting well. He was vice president of a printing company, and the deadlines were totally stressing him out. I was making enough to take care of both of us."

What Paula was really telling her second husband was that she was strong enough for both of them. He didn't need to hold himself together enough to hold down a job. He had the leisure to use drugs as much as he liked. And the unconscious payoff for Paula was that she would be the one in charge again.

"Why did he leave you?" I asked.

"His company wouldn't take him back when he was ready to start work again," she said. "He found another job two hours away, but I just couldn't stand him being gone all the time, out the door at five in the morning and not home until ten at night. We argued about it a lot. He got paranoid and started accusing me of trying to sabotage his career. Then he moved near work and told me he'd be back on weekends. We drifted further and further apart after that."

When a recovering addict finds a job that motivates him enough to commute four hours a day round-trip, there's only one thing to say: "Congratulations. You're on the right road." But for Paula, the fact that her husband was back on his feet was good news and bad news. What guarantee did she have that he still needed her and wouldn't try to control her?

When Paula met her third husband, he was recently divorced, like she was. He felt abandoned, like she did. And since his ex-father-in-law had fired him, he was out of a job and short on funds. He needed someone to help him out. And that need was nearly irresistible to Paula.

Why? Paula had been hurt as a little girl by her father—a powerful, controlling man. She had never expressed her sadness or anger about that fact and had, instead, comforted herself with the fiction that her parents had the "perfect marriage" and that she had a "fairy tale" existence as her dad's "princess." And since that fiction kept her from facing her pain, she could never move beyond it. She felt as vulnerable as a seven- or eight-year-old.

Paula was still held in pathological orbit by the gravitational pull of her past. Deep down, she believed she could find safety only in the arms of men who gave her every reassurance they were incapable of running her life. The trouble was that the only men who passed her test were also incapable of running their own lives.

The pain Paula had experienced living with a father who did not allow her to be a person had stayed buried for decades, then been reborn as the pain of two divorces and a third marriage that ended with her husband's suicide.

What terrible poetry it is that a woman with unresolved rage about growing up in her father's home would play a role in creating a fatherless one for her own little girl.

It bears repeating: the attempt to keep your pain buried will, in and of itself, lead you to resurrect it, in one form or another, again and again.

During our next session, I began digging for Paula's buried treasure. "When was the first time you screamed at your father?" I asked Paula.

She smiled. "Never. That wouldn't have gone over very well."

"You never yelled at him? Not even as a teenager?"

"No."

"What would have happened?"

"I have no idea. I wouldn't want to find out."

Paula hadn't used the past tense to express her fear—as in, "I wouldn't *have wanted* to find out." Her comment was in the present tense. She was still frightened. "Well, let's think about it together," I said.

She shrugged.

"Would he have yelled back at you?" I asked.

"Probably."

"Grounded you?"

"Like, forever."

I nodded, waited a few moments, then asked, "Hit you?"

"Maybe," she said softly, sounding more like a child than a thirty-nine-year-old woman.

She looked as though she had more to say. "What else?" I asked her.

"You don't get it. He'd have absolutely killed me." A nervous laugh. "Literally."

Exactly right. To a child, trying to appease a powerful, military-minded, emotionally distant male authority figure could certainly feel like a matter of life and death. And Paula might "literally" have spent her childhood struggling with unconscious anxiety (irrational as it may have been) that failing to follow her father's rigid demands might just get her killed. The problem was that she had never faced those childhood fears and overcome them. And that meant she was destined to continue seeing any strong man as the gravest kind of threat.

That story made sense to me. It had internal consistency and seemed to explain the events that had unfolded in Paula's life story. It seemed *true*. And that gave me the confidence to predict that Paula would come to see me as a threat, too. After all, as her doctor, I was an instant authority figure.

It was only a few sessions later, in fact, when Paula accused me of "bullying" her by pushing her to tell me more and more about the times her father had lost his temper. Those times, it turned out, had occasionally included him using a strap on her and her brother.

"I swear, you just like to hear about people's pain," she said.

"I like to hear people's truth," I replied.

"Well, it feels like being strong-armed."

If Paula was confusing me with her father, that wasn't necessarily a bad thing. She could vent her underlying feelings toward him in the safety of my office, using me as a stand-in. I decided to push her. "My office, my rules."

"I'm paying the bill," she said.

"You're always free to go somewhere else."

"Maybe you could just try backing off a little," she said.

"Or maybe I could just start drinking or using drugs so I'm not too much of a threat."

"Don't bother. You don't scare me."

"I'm just wondering what I need to do for you to feel comfortable."

"You want to make me comfortable?" she seethed. "Drop dead."

There. That comment felt as if it were mined directly from Paula's reservoirs of childhood rage. "Is that what you wished?" I asked. "That he'd die?"

"Who?"

"Your father."

She stared at me for several seconds.

"I promise I've heard a lot worse," I said.

She looked away. When she looked back at me, her eyes had filled up with tears.

"Just tell me," I said.

A minute or so later, she did. "When I was little, like seven or eight, I remember praying he'd just get sick and die," she told me. "I haven't thought of that in . . . forever." She started tearing up again. "Who would think such a thing?"

A little girl might. A really frightened little girl. And that little girl was in my office. She was the one who had tried to find adult love with broken men who would do her no harm. She was the one who had finally come out of hiding, with all her sadness and guilt, after one of those men *actually did get sick and die.*

"The kind of person who would think that kind of thing," I told Paula, "is someone who felt as if her own life were at risk—at least emotionally. Was it?"

That question opened up a discussion that lasted many more weeks, as Paula explored her early feelings of trying to please a man who was never pleased, trying to comply with rules designed more for a soldier than a child, trying to pretend she was a princess in a castle when she was more like a prisoner of war.

Paula's grief and guilt slowly resolved. About a year later, she called me as she was beginning to date again. "I'm trying to screen out all the basket cases," she said. "The trouble is, the men who seem to have it together are all so boring."

That was the same sort of reaction my patient Maggie had had (chapter five), and it is common to women and men who stop living their pathologies and start living their truth. Remember the caution I issued at the beginning of this chapter: nothing can compete energetically with the demons we have stored away since childhood; we remember them, after all, with a child's heart and mind.

The toxic dynamics we have buried will retain some of their magnetic force for many years after digging them up. Recognizing them is the key to resisting them.

"You may not gravitate naturally toward stable men," I told her. "What you went through with your dad was very charged psychologically. If you look for something as powerful as that, you're likely to end up with something just as complicated and, ultimately, just as painful. Let yourself be bored for a little while. See if it develops into something else."

Paula's fourth marriage was to someone who was, as far as I could tell, her equal intellectually, professionally, and financially. He wasn't an alcoholic or on drugs. His life wasn't a series of calamities. He also didn't make her heart race every time she laid eyes on him. What she experienced in his presence was something very different: she said she felt "at ease." I couldn't help thinking that those were the words officers in the military (like Paula's father) use to let soldiers know they can be themselves—finally.

"He really doesn't need me," she said. "That part's hard getting adjusted to. But there's an upside."

"What's that?" I asked.

"I'm pretty sure he loves me. I can't figure out why else he'd want to hang around with me."

That's the point. No recycled, negative drama from the past was holding Paula's new husband in her orbit. Love was.

What painful part of your childhood are you reproducing today (e.g., are you putting up with emotional abuse from your spouse because you got used to being criticized relentlessly by a parent you desperately needed as a child)?

_____

_____

_____

_____

_____

What painful dynamic are you running from by trying to avoid anything that reminds you of it (e.g., are you so wary of any criticism that reminds you of your hypercritical parents that you turn your back on anyone who questions you in any way)?

_____

_____

_____

_____

_____

PAINFUL INTRUSIONS FROM THE PAST

When we begin living the truth, we clear the way for healthier, happier relationships (not to mention freeing up vast stores of energy and unleashing our intellectual and creative potential). We can start living brand-new chapters of our life stories that are relatively free of the much-earlier conflicts that would otherwise predetermine the plot. We can own our futures instead of being owned by our pasts.

In my practice and my personal life, I have found that all negative patterns of behavior and emotion are due to unexamined pain from the past intruding into the present.

When people commit to finding and feeling that pain, they invariably learn they can not only survive it but benefit from it. They learn that their pain, from which they have tried so hard to run, is indeed their true source of power.

A patient of mine named Mike, twenty-seven, shows how unexamined pain from the past can fuel conditions that might seem to have little to do with one's life story.

Mike was an assistant district attorney. He came to see me with crippling symptoms of obsessive-compulsive disorder, or OCD. For years, he had been meticulous about keeping his home clean and his clothing and car perfect, but over the past several months he had developed much more severe symptoms. Driving to work, going to the mall, or heading out on a date, he would begin worrying (obsessive thinking) that he had left the stove on or a candle burning back at his house. He couldn't get the thought out of his mind. So he would double back home (compulsive behavior) to check that all was well. But then, after leaving the house a second time, he would be gripped by another obsessive worry—maybe he had left the coffeemaker on or the toaster plugged in, or he had ignored the smell of smoke as he was walking out the door.

"It's gotten to the point," he said, "where it can take me an hour or two to get from home to work. And it should be a fifteen-minute drive. I make sure I leave the house really early, but I'm still late half the time. And even once I do get in, I can't always concentrate. I can barely resist going home again to make sure the place hasn't burned down. As far as socializing, forget about it. It doesn't take women very long to figure out there's something wrong. I'm not really with them, even when I'm with them physically. My mind is back home."

Mike's symptoms were eroding his self-esteem. "I'm the one everybody else used to rely on at work to be organized and keep things moving. I can't come close to playing that role anymore. I literally move in circles half the time."

Pure neuroscientists might argue that Mike was suffering from a deficiency of the brain chemical messenger serotonin. Pure behavioral therapists might tell Mike that he should "teach" himself not to obsess by punishing himself whenever an intrusive thought should come to mind, perhaps by snapping a rubber band worn on his wrist. Pure geneticists might assert that the trigger for his disorder was encoded in his DNA from birth, and was now being fully expressed. But I believe that we are more than our neurotransmitters, more than our behavioral reflexes, and more than our genes. I believe we are all living, breathing stories and that all psychological suffering, even when it comes with a label such as OCD or ADD, has *meaning*.

That's why, although Mike was focused on describing his ob- sessions and compulsions, I was intent on going deeper. I knew I needed to search for whatever had set those obsessions and com- pulsions in motion — for the real source of his pain.

Obsessive thoughts and compulsive behaviors were, after all, keeping Mike's mind very busy. Distracted. And I didn't think that was an accident. I believed there was something Mike's mind was running away from.

Since Mike's obsession involved the destruction of his home, my first question related to early, sudden loss. "Did your life change suddenly in any way when you were a child?" I asked.

"Like my parents divorcing or something?"

"You tell me."

"I don't think so," he said.

"You didn't lose anyone you loved when you were a boy?"

He shook his head.

"Did your parents go through any sudden changes in their finances? Did you move from one town to another?"

"No."

"So nothing threatened to 'burn down' your life as you knew it," I said, making the metaphor plain. "It was pretty much smooth sailing."

He shrugged. "Pretty much. My sister was sick for a while, but . . . I mean, she got better and everything, so I don't think it would have been that."

Whenever someone shares a thought, then disavows it, you can almost count on it being very important.

I simply gave Mike's words back to him. "Your sister was sick for a while . . ."

"Yeah," he said. "She had cancer."

I felt myself grow calmer and more centered. I was moving closer to the real source of Mike's suffering, being held by the gravity of his truth. "How old was she?"

"Seven."

"So you were . . . how old?"

"Ten."

"What do you remember about it?"

"I try not to think about it," he said.

Even if it means, he could have said, *driving around in circles.* "I can understand why," I said. "But it could be very helpful for you to get in touch with your feelings from back then."

He nodded.

"Can you tell me how you found out she was sick?" I asked.

"You mean, what her symptoms were?" Mike said.

"No," I replied. "I meant, how did you find out? Who told you?"

"My dad."

"Where and how?"

"I don't know who sounds more like a district attorney, you or me."

Mike's statement may have been in jest, but it reflected a core truth. Part of Mike's job and mine was burrowing to get the truth, often from people loath to give it up. The difference was that people sitting in my office (as opposed to those on a witness stand) were withholding the truth not only from me but from themselves. And they were doing so despite the fact that divulging it would, far from getting them locked up, actually set them free. "Here's the good news," I told Mike. "The only thing you can be convicted of here is being human."

Mike smiled at that. Then he looked away and squinted, like so many of my patients do when peering back into the early chapters of their life stories. "He came to watch me during my basketball practice, which was weird, you know? Because it started right after school, at three o'clock. And he worked until six every day. So I remember feeling strange, just having this really bad feeling the whole time he was in the stands, watching. He was smiling and stuff, but the smile didn't look *real*." He sighed. "Then when I got a basket and turned around to see his reaction, he was crying."

My own heart fell just from hearing that story, which testified to the kind of impact it would have had on a ten-year-old living it. Although he had denied it when asked, Mike's life had indeed changed suddenly during his childhood. And he had never forgotten the exact moment. "Do you remember what you thought when you looked at him in the stands?" I asked.

"You might not believe this," Mike said.

"Try me."

"I didn't think anything. I didn't look at him the rest of the game. I just kept playing."

That was both believable and understandable. A ten-year-old boy who sees his father in tears can be excused for turning away, wishing that whatever has caused his father to leave work early and come find him, whatever is making his father break down into tears, would just disappear.

"When the game was over, I walked to the car with him," Mike went on. "We didn't say anything on the way. We got inside, but he just sat there without starting it. Then he told me."

"What did he say?"

"He said, 'Katie is' . . ." He stopped.

I waited.

"He said, 'Katie is sicker than we thought. She's going to have to stay in the hospital for a while.'"

A while turned out to be nearly two months, during which Katie had an abdominal tumor removed, suffered complications from the surgery, and began chemotherapy.

Mike watched as she grew more and more frail during her treatment. She lost her hair. Painful sores in her mouth made it difficult for her to eat.

Mike's parents had less time for him; they were consumed with getting Katie the care she needed. The pressure made them argue much more. Mike's father became melancholy and withdrawn.

There was nothing Mike could do about any of it. He didn't have the power to stop his sister's disease or assure himself of his parents' continuing devotion to him or bring harmony back into his home.

But something even more fundamental to his existence had changed for Mike forever. The illusions that his family was secure, that life was predictable, and that death only happened to old people had been shattered. And no one talked to him about any of it.

Mike's obsessive-compulsive symptoms, it turned out, began around that time. He would check light switches half a dozen times to make sure he had turned them off. He felt compelled to knock twice for luck on the doorjamb of his house before leaving each day for school. And he developed a nervous tic—rocking back and forth in his seat at school.

As explored in chapter three, the human mind does what it needs to do to protect itself from unbearable realities. As a ten-year-old, Mike wasn't prepared to face the possibility that his sister might die and that his family as he knew it might cease to exist. So he buried it under a mountain of silence and obsessive thoughts and compulsive behaviors. If he could just keep the lights from burning down the house, he would be in control, at least of something.

The obsessions and compulsions never went away. They went through cycles, getting better and worse. Now they were nearly unbearable.

It was certainly the case that Mike might be helped by medicine, and I prescribed one with a good track record of reducing the symptoms of OCD. But I also sat with Mike for several weeks, helping him talk about his gut-level fears from when he was ten, his terror when his sister's cancer recurred when she was thirteen, and his grief when, shortly thereafter, his beloved family pet—a dog—died suddenly.

"I couldn't even show he really mattered to me," Mike said. "It would have seemed weird, with everything my sister was going through."

"Did you love him?"

"What kid doesn't love his dog?"

"I asked about you."

His eyes filled up, and he nodded. "He was great," he said. "Barney. Honestly, if it weren't for him, I don't know how I would have gotten through that time. I loved him a lot."

Is it too much to wonder whether even Mike's choice of careers—focused on knowing the details of every case, enforcing the rules, and *protecting* the community—had been motivated by being so vulnerable as a child?

But here's the problem: nothing could have protected Mike's sister from getting cancer. Nothing can imprison death. Only Mike being willing to feel his vulnerability (and that of everyone close to him) held the promise of him coming to terms with it. Only truly looking back at his father weeping in the stands at his basketball game, fresh from hearing that Mike's sister had cancer, could turn that event into something he had survived instead of something he would keep running from for the rest of his life.

"It would be great if checking the stove and the coffeemaker and all the candles in your house would keep tragedy away from you," I told him. "But that won't work. You can drive back and forth from your house all day, every day, making sure it hasn't burned down, but that won't stop cancer. All it'll do is keep you from living your own life."

The combination of medicine and counseling helped Mike abandon his shield of obsessions and compulsions. "I figure," he told me, "that even if it costs me my house, I'm not driving back to check anything. Let it burn down, if that's what's going to happen. Because I can't let it destroy everything else I have" — he looked directly at me — "not after realizing how much I went through to get here. And you know I'm not talking about law school."

By looking directly at his pain, Mike was able to put it in the past, where it belonged. He was able to step out of the role of trying to control the future. That didn't mean he would be immune to sadness about his sister's struggle with cancer or the loss of his beloved pet or the period of discord in his parents' marriage. Much to the contrary, it meant that he would be in touch with those feelings. And as a result, he would no longer be hostage to them.

I wish I had had more control over my life as a child or adolescent when:
(*Example: "I wish I had had more control over my life as a child or adolescent when* my parents took me out of public school and registered me for parochial school. I wasn't doing well in classes because my creativity was being stifled, and it only got worse in an even more structured environment."*)

_____

_____

_____

_____

_____

If I could have edited out one event from my early life experiences, it would have been:
(*Example:* "*If I could have edited out one event from my early life experiences, it would have been* the day my parents adopted a third child. It isn't that I don't love him, but he needed a great deal of their attention, and I have to admit I felt pushed aside.")

_____

_____

_____

_____

_____

REVEALING YOUR OWN PATTERNS

Mike's and Paula's experiences are examples of the fact that denial is a losing strategy, because the magnetic pull of the underlying pain is so incredibly strong. The walls around our intimate truths that we build as fortresses to "protect" us ultimately become our personal prisons, stifling our chances to be fully alive, unscripted, spontaneous, real—and free.

In the space below, or in your notebook, write down the patterns you see throughout your life. Think about both your personal and your professional life, and what situations you seem to find yourself in again and again.

About your personal life, ask yourself questions such as:

- Do I keep dating people who consistently lie to me?
- Do I drop everything for my friends and never get anything back from them?
- Am I attracted to people who need to be "taken care of"?
- Am I attracted to people who promise to take care of me?

Make a list of how these or any other patterns you display in relationships consistently show up in your life:

_____

_____

_____

_____

_____

_____

About your professional life, ask yourself questions such as:

- Are you the one at work who always takes the fall for anything that goes wrong?
- Do you always manage to land a great job, only to "blow it" within a few weeks or months?
- Do you often allow others to take credit for your ideas or hard work?
- Do you often take credit for other people's ideas or hard work?

Make a list of how these or any other patterns repeat themselves in your professional life:

_____

_____

_____

_____

_____

_____

Are you being held in pathological orbit, repeating the same negative patterns again and again? Whatever your patterns are, they aren't accidents. They aren't random. Their trajectories are defined by painful chapters of your early life history that you are trying to avoid. It's no different from driving a car with a blind spot in your field of vision. The blind spot will define your journey and consume more and more of your time and energy, because it will result in accident after accident.

Dwell a little on the patterns you identify in your own life, and try to explain to yourself what events in your earlier life experience may have set them in motion. What painful realizations about your life could these patterns be helping you to avoid?

For instance, if your pattern is that you consistently date people who lie to you, ask yourself, "Who in my early life was a liar? To whom did he or she lie? How did his or her lying affect my life?"

What events early in my life may have set my patterns in motion?

_____

_____

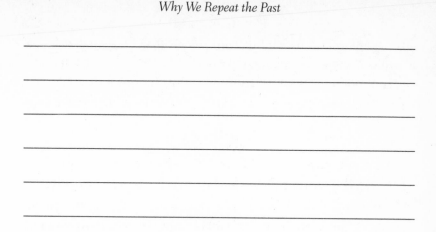

START LINKING YOUR PAST TO YOUR PRESENT

The greatest promise for personal growth is looking in the mirror in order to see behind you, because tying your specific problems to their roots in the past allows you to see how the painful chapters in your life story are holding you hostage to self-defeating patterns of thought and behavior.

Although it may be difficult, I ask you again to become an investigator of your own life history, a person in relentless pursuit of the truth, convinced the mystery of your suffering can be solved by looking in the mirror you've exposed by lowering your shields. Write a compelling story that explains why you find yourself facing the specific problems you listed in the previous chapters. For example, broken marriages often have their roots in strained early relationships with parents—or between parents. Depression fueling alcohol abuse often has its roots in feelings of being unloved, unwanted, or powerless. Being abused physically or emotionally today often means that one got used to being physically or emotionally abused long ago.

If you're living a life story that has veered into pain, then there is pain in much earlier chapters. Where?

Go back to the reason you bought this book. Suppose your reason was because of a troubled relationship—you're in a stressful marriage with a husband you suspect of infidelity. Think about other relationships you've had in the past. Have you experienced infidelity before? To understand the roots of your relationship patterns, begin by asking yourself questions about your early life:

- Do you know if your father cheated on your mother?
- Did you suspect that your father was cheating on your mother?
- Did your father remarry within months of your mother's death or of your parents' divorce, leaving open the question of whether he was unfaithful before her absence?
- Did your mother ever confide that she suspected your father of being unfaithful?
- Did you learn that your mother was herself unfaithful?
- Were you inappropriately seduced by a married man at a very young age?

Any of these situations may have been the trigger that set your relationship patterns in motion.

Solving the Mystery of Your Own Life Story

This is where you truly begin to make sense of how the past is influencing you today. Write your narrative here or in your notebook. Write whatever comes to you in the moment. Don't worry if you can't "figure everything out" on your first try. Even Columbo had to go over the facts again and again until he could see how everything fit together. Now you must be your own Columbo, searching through the clues of your life. There is no right or wrong way to do this. It's your story—write it any way you want. Just be certain that it links your current problem(s) with what you experienced much earlier in your life.

_____

_____

_____

_____

_____

_____

_____

_____

_____

_____

_____

_____

_____

_____

After you've written down a narrative that makes sense of your suffering, read it to yourself. Feel free to revise it over the next few days, making it truer and truer to your gut feelings about what happened to set the stage for your suffering.

I will ask you to write your narrative several more times as you go through this book and gather more clues to your life story. Those clues will be revealed as you complete the exercises in each chapter. As you may have already realized, these exercises have been designed to build one upon the other until you have a pretty clear picture of your true self. One important note: if at any point in the process you are overwhelmed by the insights you're uncovering, you may want to contact a therapist for support. The point of this whole book is to help you realize that you are not alone, and that you do not need to continue to live in pain. I urge you to take whatever steps are necessary to lead you to a happier, more truthful life.

Thomas Merton, the great monk and poet, said, "The truth that many people never understand, until it is too late, is that the more you try to avoid suffering the more you suffer."

Now here's the exciting part: blind spots in your life don't have to be forever. You can break out of the pathological, limiting orbit defined by your past. You just have to turn in the direction of your pain and keep your eyes wide open.

CHAPTER 7

Are We Hardwired to Run From Pain?

Why is it so hard to face the difficult truths about our lives and grow from them? One reason is that the human impulse to avoid painful emotional realities seems to be hardwired into our nervous systems.

During the 1950s, psychologist Richard Solomon proved that dogs trained to avoid physical pain (and the emotional suffering that comes with it) never abandon the evasive strategies they learn, even when those strategies have outlived their usefulness.

In Solomon's classic *anticipatory-avoidance learning* experiment, a dog was confined to a cage in which half the floor was electrified. A buzzer was sounded just before an electrical shock was delivered. The dog quickly learned to jump to the other side of the cage—just at the sound of the buzzer. And once the dog had learned this behavior, it occurred each and every time he heard the buzzer, *even though no shock was ever given again.*

Presumably, the dog's nervous system had gone on autopilot. No shock was being paired with the buzzer anymore, but the dog never tested whether he could stop panicking and just sit still. His brain seemed intent on never taking that risk again. Running away was now a neurological reflex reaction based on *past suffering.*

People show the same anticipatory-avoidance of emotional pain. When we feel let down as children by those close to us, we may "jump" away from real intimacy as adults, never again risking the "shock" of disappointment or betrayal or abandonment again. And this anticipatory-avoidance reflex deprives us of learning that the world can offer us much more than our childhoods did.

Isn't that, after all, Maggie's story from chapter five? Having been hurt deeply by her father's known and repeated infidelities, she had never truly trusted that another man would help rather than harm her. It was as though the hardwired memory of what it felt like to be betrayed as a young girl had led her to keep running forever from potential male mentors and possible true love.

Isn't that Tom's story? Having paired the memory of what it felt like to lose his home and his education with his father's risk-taking behavior, his mind seemed to have gone on autopilot, running away from every risk, even the manageable one of following his heart and opening a restaurant.

Now here are the questions that should stop you from turning pages for a few minutes: Is this your story? Is your emotional life on autopilot? Are you running from the truth, avoiding situations that remind you of it (consciously or unconsciously), even though doing so costs you your potential for growth and true happiness?

If your life is on autopilot, are you ready to do the work of unearthing the early disappointments that preprogrammed your own emotional reflexes? Are you ready to begin living the truth?

THE BRAIN'S SURVIVAL STRATEGIES

One reason that this takes work is that the human brain seems anatomically equipped to bury specific memories of what caused us pain in childhood while "remembering" and reproducing the techniques we used to avoid it.

We emotionally run away from things that remind us of our traumas without knowing why.

According to psychology professor Lynn Nadel and others, recent research suggests that the parts of the brain involved in maintaining patterns of behavior are different from those involved in recalling events. Emotional skills and habits we acquire seem to reside in the cerebellum, basal ganglia, and amygdala. Memories of events seem to reside in the hippocampus.

The hippocampus can literally "forget" or suppress exactly what a person lived through, while the amygdala "remembers" very well how badly it felt and perpetuates the mental gymnastics that were used to make the pain stop.

This means we can live like children who, having stepped on nails (a memory lost in the hippocampus), resolve to never walk again (a behavioral pattern permanently encoded in the amygdala).

Why does the hippocampus forget the real source of our suffering? We've already gone over one reason: temporarily denying or burying the traumas we live through as children may be necessary to survive emotionally. Another reason is that memory circuits in the hippocampus are not fully developed in children, while those in the amygdala are. Moreover, the nerve cells that make up memory circuits in the hippocampus are extremely sensitive to stress. Research has shown that stress causes the adrenal glands to release cortisol into the bloodstream, and high levels of cortisol are toxic to the hippocampus and can actually cause the cells there to wither and die.

Think about that. It means that the stress of being emotionally abused by your older sister as a little girl can change your brain and make it harder to remember the abusive experiences you lived through. But the sadness and fear you experienced because of her, as well as the strategies you adopted to avoid being hurt by her, don't fade. And that makes it very hard to put blame exactly where it belongs and learn that the world might be different from the way it was at home.

An analogy: You are watching a movie in which a teenage girl emotionally tortures her little sister. The movie is so graphic that you get up and leave the cinema. But upon returning to your car, you forget the specific content of the film and, no longer remembering the single female character who sparked such strong emotions in you, are left with extreme distrust of all teenage girls.

The potential imbalance of power between the hippocampus and the amygdala is only one biological hurdle in the way of abandoning the fiction in our lives and seeing reality. The groundbreaking research and thinking of neuroscientist Candace Pert, PhD, who worked alongside one of my own mentors at Johns Hopkins, Solomon Snyder, MD, PhD, makes it plain that our minds and bodies work in concert as a selective filter of our experiences, keeping us from questioning our preconceived notions about ourselves and others. How? *Neuropeptides,* the chemicals relaying messages between nerve cells in the brain, also turn out to affect many other organs in the body. This means our emotions, our senses, and our bodies are intimately linked. When we encounter danger, for example, we not only experience the emotion of fear but prepare to either fight or flee, with our hearts pumping more vigorously and our oxygen intake increasing and glucose flowing out of cells and into our bloodstreams. Our eyes may be directed toward or away from whatever has frightened us. Our irises may expand to let in more light or contract to let in less. We may tremble or feel our stomachs sinking.

In her book *Molecules of Emotion,* Pert makes the compelling case that these integrated "bodymind" reactions are altered by previous experience. One's entire being—brain, gut, heart, and six senses—is trained by what one has lived through to screen out certain events and perceptions and to screen in others.

As Pert puts it, "In order for the brain not to be overwhelmed by the constant deluge of sensory input, some sort of filtering system must enable us to pay attention to what our bodymind deems the most important pieces of information and to ignore the others. . . . What we perceive as real is filtered along a gradient of past emotions and learning."

What we respond to and how we respond to it depends *neurologically* on what we have concluded about the world in the past, *even if our conclusions were based on single, painful interactions and have completely outlived their usefulness.*

In Maggie's case, for example, a male employer worthy of her trust might have gone unnoticed by her. She might literally have "looked away" from his warm smile or reassuring glance, literally not heard the kind tone in his voice, while focusing in an unbalanced way on subtle signs of impatience or irritability or anything resembling a broken promise (even a canceled appointment or delayed personal evaluation). Then, armed with "evidence" telling her nervous system that she was with a disappointing man just like her father, her heart might race, her eyes might fill with tears, and reflex escape strategies based in childhood disappointment might be set in motion. Maybe she would stop trying to bond with him or impress him, maybe she would let her resentment of him start to show, or maybe she would begin planning to escape to another job.

When Maggie met the truly deceitful woman who ultimately

hired her, her "bodymind" likely responded as it did to her mother, with feelings of comfort and affection. So she took the job the woman offered her, essentially running from her "shocking" father to her "safe" mother.

The trouble is that Maggie's mind and body were operating in concert on faulty information based on a reticence to feel pain and see the truth. Maggie wasn't really safe with her mother when she was a girl, and she wasn't any safer with her employer as an adult. It just felt that way—in every way.

When we try to rid ourselves of the fictional aspects of our life stories, we are up against intertwined emotional and physical roadblocks.

Luckily, confronting reality, being willing to feel our pain and achieve new insights, not only changes us psychologically but neurologically as well. Pert writes: "Fortunately . . . [neuropeptide] receptors are not stagnant, and can change in both sensitivity and in the arrangement they have with other proteins in the cell membrane. This means that even if we are 'stuck' emotionally, fixated on a version of reality that does not serve us well, there is always a biochemical potential for change and growth." And that's why, as human beings who can reason and choose the courageous path of truth, we can do better than Solomon's dogs.

WHEN HARDWIRING MEETS EMOTIONAL CONFLICT

Back when I was starting my residency training in psychiatry, I worked with a man whose problems initially seemed to be caused entirely by injuries to his brain. He was one of the first people who made me curious about the complex ways the mind can affect anatomy and physiology—and vice versa.

Johnathan was a forty-seven-year-old white man, with a history of a stroke five years before. He had been admitted to the psychiatry unit after coming to the emergency room with suicidal thoughts and a very high blood alcohol level. His vague chief complaint was that he had not been the same since the bleeding in his brain.

That short medical summary, however, entirely missed important parts of Johnathan's story. His simple explanation wouldn't satisfy a reader's need to understand the inner workings of a character, and it shouldn't have satisfied my need to understand him as a patient.

What struck me first about him was that he looked like a pudgy but obviously powerful forty-seven-year-old boy with a crew cut. He spoke quietly, seemingly without emotion, even when talking about pain or love. He told me he was depressed and anxious and couldn't sleep because of nightmares. He didn't feel like eating. The only visible hint of despair came when he mentioned that his girlfriend had started to insist he propose marriage.

But was the hint of pain I thought I saw in my patient's face my own invention? Was it his fear of commitment to one woman, or a reflection of my own? And why should such musings feel as if they were an interruption in his case history rather than at the very heart of it?

Johnathan was neither homicidal nor paranoid. He denied experiencing any hallucinations. He was alert and knew the date and the name of the hospital. His concentration was not impaired, his attention span was normal, and his memory was intact.

He had started drinking as a youngster. He stole his first beer from a store and still remembered the alcohol making him feel fearless, like a gangster. He drank more and more throughout his teens—up to a case of beer a day.

During the early 1960s, Johnathan first experienced what he called "wild anxiety." Although he didn't relate the two, the anxiety happened to start when he proposed to a woman he had met in college. All of a sudden he couldn't work, sleep, or eat. He left the woman, increased his drinking, and started hearing voices that told him to kill himself. The voices went away after he spent a few weeks alone.

Then, following another failed relationship in the mid-1980s, the right side of his thalamus, a part of the brain that plays a major role in regulating emotion, started to bleed.

The scientist in me knew the questions raised by that stroke. Did my patient suffer high blood pressure? Had an aneurysm burst? Were the arteries and veins in his brain malformed since birth?

But was it folly for the healer in me to wonder first about a connection between lost loves and stroke, about emotions disrupting anatomy? Why dismiss my quiet suspicion that this patient's conflicted emotional state could have worked his thalamus into such a frenzy that the little blood vessels supplying it burst?

His family history was negative for cerebrovascular disease. What I noted was that Johnathan didn't trust his father, an abusive man who drank excessively and frequently left home in the middle of the night.

"Where was your dad going?" I once asked.

"I don't know," Johnathan said.

"Did he work nights?"

"Who knows? Maybe he had a woman. So what?"

I let the issue drop. What did it have to do, after all, with his broken brain?

I should have asked much more about it. I also should have asked more about my patient's mother and the women he had left. I should have ferreted out how his new girlfriend's desire for a commitment was related to his symptoms. But I was new then at treating patients. I was caught up in the technical scientific debate in the psychiatry unit over whether Johnathan had bipolar disorder or a clear-cut case of major depression, and whether to prescribe the antidepressant Prozac or desipramine. I was not seeing him as a person, with a life story that was more than just a clinical history.

I eventually prescribed two antidepressants, because a combination often can fight depression better than any one medication alone. And in about three weeks, Johnathan seemed less sad. He had stopped talking about hurting himself. He was sleeping and eating. But he still kept saying, "It's like I have this spot inside me that I'd like to rub, 'cause it hurts, but I can't get at it." And maybe because I didn't want to go there, didn't want to dig deep into his past and stir up his pain, I didn't ask any more about it. I just increased his medicine.

I doubt that spot ever really left him. Maybe it had something to do with his father's philandering. Maybe that unconscious lesson had partly set up my patient to run from women who might otherwise have had his complete allegiance. And I know now that no amount of Prozac or desipramine could have changed that pattern or protected his brain from the razor-sharp emotions coursing through it. Only getting to the truth could have.

As I have learned, the answer to the question "Are we hardwired to suffer?" is yes and no. Biological forces work to protect us, to help us forget the traumas of childhood. The bad news is that these biological forces also set in motion behaviors that may keep us from living happy, fulfilled lives. But the good news is that by working to uncover the sources of our childhood traumas, we can literally change not just the content of our minds but also the molecular architecture of our brains. We can free ourselves—*psychologically and neurologically*—to see things we did not see, feel things we did not feel, and live lives we could not even imagine.

I have learned since working with Johnathan that this journey is always possible. The early chapters of our life stories may be buried in the hippocampus or shrouded in denial, but they are never completely lost. When we are determined to reopen them and have the tools to do so, we can read them with an adult's mind instead of a child's, and move beyond them.

To be clear, I believe that psychiatric medications have their place. They are powerful and effective tools to help stabilize a person's thought processes and emotions while he or she does the hard work of digging deep for the truth. The trouble is that too many psychiatrists never motivate patients to commit to that hard work, seemingly content to use medications to bolster their brain chemistry. In so doing, they can easily be complicit in keeping their patients' real-life stories from surfacing. They miss the fact that, as the late *New York Times Book Review* editor Anatole Broyard wrote in the article "Doctor, Talk to Me" (August 26, 1990), "Inside every patient, there's a poet trying to get out."

SHORT-CIRCUIT YOUR HARDWIRING

I want to keep motivating you to pursue your truth as you read this book, so that once you reach part three, your mind and heart will be as open as possible to living the truth.

So I ask you now to continue to short-circuit your hard-wiring and add more to the life story you wrote in the previous chapter. To that end, here are some more prompts you can complete to help you get beyond the pain in which you currently reside:

If people knew everything about me, the thing that might end up costing me their friendship or affection or respect would be:

_____

_____

_____

_____

_____

The reason I think that revelation would be so troubling to people is:

_____

_____

_____

_____

_____

But if I were going to try to tell any person everything about me, I would tell:

_____

I would choose that person because:

_____

_____

_____

_____

_____

CHAPTER 8

Understanding the
Family Fiction

In chapter three, we learned that we often create fictional life stories for ourselves as a means of coping with (or actually denying) painful episodes of our early lives. We put up a variety of shields to protect ourselves from these memories. And you are not alone in the process of fictionalizing your past. In fact, the vast majority of families, like individuals, have partly fictional histories to which they cling to insulate one or more family members from painful realities. Fear of the real story can be magnified several times because the truth would deprive many individuals the false comfort of denial.

It may be that continuing to believe in the family fiction is holding you back from living your truth. In order to get to that truth, you may have to consult several sources. But before you do, you need to understand how family fictions work.

YOUR FAMILY'S THEME

Family fictions are often built around a central theme. For example, rather than confront the fact that a father (or grandfather) squandered his wealth through poor judgment, a family might collectively create and perpetuate the myth that he was "cheated" by a business partner who abused their friendship by being too controlling and "taking over everything." The father is held up as someone with great business skills who was simply "too trusting."

The fallout from that bit of family fiction can be widespread for children emerging into adulthood:

- The unspoken message is that Dad is too weak to face the truth. His ego must be protected, at all costs. And when a son or daughter learns to sacrifice reality to avoid hurting a father's feelings, he or she will make the same devil's bargain again—maybe for a spouse.

- Since the family cannot accept evidence that their finances could continue to worsen under his stewardship, Dad retains control of assets better handled by Mom.

- Dad is free to dispense business advice to his kids, who may be inclined to follow it to their detriment, because to do otherwise would challenge the family fiction.

- In the future, the children in the family—wary of being "cheated" like their father—might be so suspicious of business partnerships that they can't form or maintain them.

- Future marriages might even suffer if one of the children (primed to equate love with blind trust) feels that his wife (or her husband) is questioning his (or her) financial decisions.

- One of the children with genuine potential in business might shy away from it because the family fiction dictates that business "always ruins friendships."

- If a son or daughter does take a financial risk and loses money, he or she is much more likely to blame it on someone else rather than learn from the experience.

- Denial becomes the dominant emotional strategy for the family. In all matters that could spark self-reflection, the family learns to respond by closing ranks and criticizing outsiders.

This is the way that one unspeakable truth in a family creates a devastating fiction that costs more and more to sustain.

The truth—that the father in this family wasn't a very good businessman—is likely to get buried deeper and deeper as life events challenge it more and more. His next financial loss will be the occasion to prove that he was victimized yet again. It *must* be so.

NEARLY EVERY FAMILY HAS A FICTION

Family conspiracies to deny reality can be unconscious, elaborate, and very powerful. Many family members have vested interests in "forgetting" where the truth is buried.

I recently worked with a patient whose story proves this point. Linda was a slight, redheaded forty-two-year-old woman who came to see me with symptoms of major depression, including low mood, insomnia, difficulty concentrating, and decreased self-esteem. She had tolerated emotional abuse from her husband for several years and said she felt as if she had "nothing left to give." She had three sons—four, seven, and ten—whom she was always trying to protect from her husband, literally standing between him and the boys, trying to deflect or absorb his scathing criticisms of them.

"He calls them every name in the book, even in front of people," she said. "He says horrible things like, 'You should never have been born.' And it doesn't have to be for anything major. Even little things set him off, like not taking their plates to the sink, not being friendly when we have people over to the house, not wearing the 'right' clothes. But the thing is, I know he doesn't mean it."

"Why do you say that?" I asked.

"He's just burned-out a lot of the time. He works so hard. He's under a lot of pressure. And now, I'm out of commission, crying all the time. And that just makes it even harder for him—and the kids."

Linda was actually blaming herself for her husband being abusive. "What does he do for work?" I asked her.

"He's an EMT. He has to deal with horrible things. Car accidents. Heart attacks. You name it."

Among my friends are surgeons, emergency room doctors, combat veterans, and police officers. They have to deal with plenty of ugliness, too. But I've never seen them lash out at their kids in any serious or sustained way. "He says his job makes it impossible to control himself at home and in public?" I asked.

She shook her head. "He doesn't make excuses for himself. I can just tell that's what's going on for him."

Linda's husband didn't have to make excuses for himself. Linda was doing it for him.

"You can tell by the fact that he loses his temper?" I asked her.

"That, and other stuff. He gets to a point where he just shuts down. I know he's thinking about everything he's seen. And he drinks a lot more than he should."

We weren't fifteen minutes into our time together, and Linda had already mentioned a second reason her husband might be losing his temper—his drinking. The fact that she was letting him off the hook by blaming his stressful job made me wonder whether she was predisposed to do so by her earlier life experience. "You're very understanding," I said.

She shrugged. "My dad was a firefighter," she said. "He retired five years ago."

"He was under a lot of stress while you were growing up?"

"To say the least."

"How did he deal with it?"

"Not so well."

"Meaning?"

"Let's just say he makes my husband look tame by comparison," she said.

Whenever people use that phrase—"let's just say"—they always have much more to say. It just isn't easy to find the words, or the courage. "Your father's temper was even worse?" I asked Linda.

She nodded.

"He yelled at you? Hit you?"

She smiled for the first time since arriving at the office. "He didn't mean it. He did the best he could. He loved all of us so much."

"He did the best he could" is another shield of denial people routinely raise. Just because our parents did the best they could doesn't mean they did well enough to keep us from harm. And until we're willing to admit we suffered and didn't deserve to, we can't learn from the painful dynamics we lived through. Nor can we avoid reproducing those dynamics in the future.

I wasn't surprised Linda had somehow summoned the energy to smile as she raised her shield of denial.

"Did he drink, too?" I asked.

"Only to get to sleep," she said. "He had nightmares. That's what my mom said. We all tried to make it relaxing for him when he got home, but . . ."

"But . . ."

"There's only so much you can do to settle someone down who's been running into burning buildings all day, or waiting to."

We were at the heart of the family fiction that had set the stage for Linda's selecting an angry man to marry, then forgiving his abuse of her and her children. Her mother had suggested that a man who verbally and physically abuses his family isn't to blame, that the family has the responsibility to comfort and coddle such a man rather than to confront him or flee from him, that he can have true love in his heart for his wife and children while attacking them emotionally and physically. Even the theme of alcohol abuse being a defensible way to medicate stress had been written into her life story (and that of her future family) while Linda was still a girl.

Is it any surprise that the home Linda had created was a replica of the one she had come from, where she had been valued for absorbing the rage of a man, forgiving his abuse, and trying to heal him? After all, her father supposedly really *loved* her, despite screaming at her and hitting her.

"Was your father an angry person before becoming a firefighter?" I asked.

She looked confused. "I have no idea."

"Did he drink before that?"

She shook her head. "I don't know. Why do you ask?"

I wanted to be forceful enough with Linda to begin to take down the shield of denial that was her birthright. "You're letting him off the hook for assaulting you and being drunk every night because he was out all day saving lives. So I just wanted to know if he was a violent alcoholic before he started fighting fires."

"He wasn't alcoholic. He—"

"He drank every night."

She didn't respond.

"He screamed at you and hit you."

"But . . ."

I pushed harder. "But he was running into burning buildings. Right. I get it. Just like your husband is scraping people off the pavement, so that supposedly gives him a free pass to level you and the kids with emotional abuse. But guess what? There's no excuse for hurting your wife and kids. So why don't you go and gather some facts."

"Like what?"

"Does your father have any sisters or brothers who are still alive?" I asked.

"A sister."

"Then ask her if he had trouble with alcohol or his temper *before* he became a firefighter."

"What if he did?"

"If he did, you can stop giving him a free pass on hurting you just because he was helping others. Because he was just using that as an excuse. And you can start wondering whether you chose a husband a lot like him because you don't feel valuable unless you're absorbing a man's violence."

After a lot more encouragement, Linda took me up on my offer. Her aunt told her that her dad hadn't been destroyed emotionally by fighting fires. He'd been troubled as far back as his teenage years. And here's the stunning but not surprising part (at least to me): his own father — Linda's grandfather — had been alcoholic and violent, too. And *his* wife had stayed by his side.

Three generations of women in Linda's family had defined their roles as wives and mothers in the same toxic way. Seeing that fact was the beginning of Linda's questioning the fiction she had been taught and starting to see her reality, however painful: neither her father nor her husband ever loved her the way she deserved to be loved — purely, without her having to volunteer for abuse as part of the bargain.

Only once Linda realized this was she able to start standing up for herself and her kids. She didn't begin to hate her husband or suddenly want to leave him, but she did get angry. She gradually made it plain to him that she wasn't going to be his doormat or let him abuse her kids any longer. She told him she would indeed *have to leave* if he couldn't change, starting with getting help for his alcoholism. And the most wonderful part of the story is that when he did get help, he gave her some real evidence that he actually did value her, that she had the power to insist on a better life for her and her children.

You have that power, too. Armed with family facts rather than family fiction, you can start to write more true and powerful chapters of your own life story.

Not every family member will be as forthcoming as Linda's aunt. That's why the *way* in which you seek the truth is critical.

Do you suspect your family has a fiction? What do you think it is?

(*Example:* "I've always been told that my sister left home for a year to live with my aunt in Arizona because she needed the dry air. I believe there is more to this story that I have not been told.")

_____

_____

_____

_____

_____

SEEKING THE TRUTH FROM OTHERS

Because our life stories often veer into fiction while we are still children, finding our truth can be greatly accelerated by reaching out to others for facts that have been kept from us or which we have forgotten. But not everyone will be receptive. You need a strategy to select likely sources and then to help them help you. Here's a five-point plan:

1. *The people who are the most "together" may be the ones in the most denial.*

Often family members who are portrayed as the happiest and most successful are also the ones living behind shields of denial themselves. Families, in fact, may isolate those members who are most closely connected with and troubled by the truth. If abuse has occurred in a family, for example, the person who hasn't been willing to "forget" about it may be the one who is most obviously struggling with unwieldy moods, who is prone to anger at others in the family, or who is shunned entirely. So those individuals are often the best ones to go to for data.

Similarly, much truth can be mined from relationships in conflict. If your father doesn't speak with his brother, that doesn't mean you can't—at least once. You can call up and say you're looking for more insight into what the trouble was between them. Maybe you'll hear the story line that your dad shared with you or maybe you'll hear something very different. And if you learn that you've been told something other than the truth, that should motivate you even more to get to the bottom of things.

2. *Remember that family fictions often reach back generations.*

Don't restrict your sources to parents, aunts, and uncles. You can look at the life stories of your grandparents and assume that the unresolved conflicts they struggled with are likely to have trickled down one or more generations. Ask your parents about your grandparents, but also ask your grandparents (on both sides) about your mother and father.

3. *Your siblings or friends may have unraveled the secrets of your life story before you.*

Some of those close to you, whether siblings or friends, may have already come up with some of the truths you're seeking about the past, the way you live your life, or the way that others contribute to or detract from your well-being. But they don't always volunteer their insights. Often you have to ask directly.

Siblings, for example, sometimes believe that the negative experiences they had with parents didn't affect you, even when they did. Or they may think that if they share with you their truthful but troubling memories, you will shy away from them. And friends may fear that if they tell you about disturbing patterns they've observed in your life, they'll lose you. So you have to ask directly for their help.

4. The person who makes you the most uncomfortable may be one of the keys to your truth.

If you've had a strained relationship with your mother, she may well be the person who can give you further insight into ways in which that relationship set the stage for difficulties you're facing now. But in order to encourage her to share that information, you have to listen to what she tells you without getting angry. Think of yourself more as a reporter, investigating your own life. Reporters listen without reacting much because that makes their interviewees feel safe telling them more and more. This leads to the next point.

5. Always ask for help in a way that is nonthreatening and not accusatory, but direct.

People respond far better to requests for help than to an attempt to make them choose sides. Always make it plain from the beginning that you're on a personal journey to try to understand *your* life better, that you really appreciate any help the person you're speaking with can give you, and that you are *not* looking to blame anyone for anything.

Also tell the person you are speaking with that whatever insights he or she offers to you will be kept completely confidential—and mean it.

Here are some suggested ways to open the discussion:

- I know this question may seem to come out of the blue, but I think you might be able to help me out. I've been trying to get a better handle lately on what my next step in life should be, which includes figuring out my strengths and weaknesses. So I was wondering if you could give me your thoughts on that and why I might have become the way I am. Like, if you saw me as too controlling or something, or too dependent on others, I'd love it if you'd just tell me that and give me some ideas about whether my family might be part of it.

- You grew up in the same house as I did. What have you figured out about how Mom and Dad affected us—positively and negatively? I never asked before, and I'll never tell anyone what you say, but I think getting to the next step in my growth as a person kind of depends on looking back at the way we grew up.

- You grew up with me (or in my neighborhood, or with my mother as your sister, or with my father as your brother). Maybe we've had similar reactions to things. What have you figured out about how these people affected *your* development?

After you speak to your "sources," write down what they've told you, because you might want to be able to reflect upon what was said, and it will be helpful to have a written record to help you remember.

_____

_____

_____

_____

_____

_____

_____

_____

_____

REVISITING YOUR LIFE STORY

Refer back to page 155 and write your life story again or add to the one you've already written, incorporating the information you've learned from others about yourself, your childhood, your family, and your family fiction.

_____

_____

_____

_____

_____

_____

_____

_____

_____

_____

_____

_____

_____

_____

WELCOMING THE TOUGH TRUTHS

Even though you are the one seeking the truth, beginning to uncover it won't necessarily feel good. In fact, you may find yourself resisting the very information you are seeking. It isn't easy hearing that your father always favored his sons, not you, his daughter. It isn't easy hearing that your mother was so focused on her own needs to ensure peace and keep up appearances that she really couldn't hear your complaints about how your brother was treating you. It isn't easy learning from a sibling that it was always pretty clear your dad was unfaithful. But facts are always the antidote to fiction, and fictional life stories always veer into trouble.

All the anger and sadness and anxiety you may experience when hearing the truth has been inside you all along, kept underground by unconscious psychological strategies that distract you—compulsive eating, obsessive thinking, alcohol abuse, repeated relationships that don't really yield the love you need. Keep an open mind and an open heart, and you will find yourself using all that wasted emotional energy to live more fully and more powerfully than ever before.

CHAPTER 9

Facing the Truth
Is Not About Blame

One of the hurdles in seeking out the pain in your past and turning it into your power is that it can feel as if you are blaming others for your misfortune, including people you love, such as your parents or siblings or grandparents. Many of my patients pause at the door of self-discovery and tell me a version of, "I don't want to make it seem like my parents are *responsible* for what I'm going through. That just seems like a cop-out." Others, like Linda, want me to know that their parents did the best they could, that they love their parents, despite their shortcomings.

These worries reflect a core misunderstanding about the ultimate goal of living the truth. Living the truth isn't only about empowering yourself by short-circuiting the human tendency to pull away from your own pain. It's about realizing that your parents and grandparents were limited by the same very human, very understandable, yet very toxic, dynamic. They did do the best they could with the psychological resources they had, whether or not it was good enough to minimize your suffering and keep you safe.

Living the truth is about forgiveness, not blame. Because any problems visited upon you during your developmental years weren't invented by your parents. They weren't invented by their parents, either. They are the result of psychological dynamics that reach back many generations, each passing along pain to the next, because no one was helped to confront it, own it, and overcome it.

THE CYCLE OF PAIN

I recently treated a twenty-one-year-old woman named Rachel whose story brings the multigenerational cycle of pain to life. Rachel was suffering from depression and cocaine addiction, and had tried to overdose on sleeping pills. She came to my office with her mother, Wendy, who had taken the entire day off from work to make it possible for Rachel to spend a few hours with me (even though she was having trouble making ends meet for herself, Rachel, and her two sons).

I met with Rachel alone. She spent the first five or ten minutes reciting her symptoms in great detail. They were classic ones for major depression, including low self-esteem, low energy, disturbed sleep, lack of interest in the acting classes she once loved, sudden tearfulness, and lack of appetite. It was clear she had been trying to treat those symptoms with cocaine. But her diagnoses—major depression and cocaine dependence—were really just labels for her suffering. They didn't tell me anything about *why* she was suffering.

In fact, as she detailed the number of hours she had slept each of the nights the previous week and exactly how little she had eaten the prior few days, I felt as though she were using her laundry list of symptoms as a shield to stop me from getting to know her — as if she were trying to transport me into her world of *not* feeling.

I wasn't about to go there. "Tell me the most painful part of your life," I interrupted.

"You mean the worst part of being depressed — not sleeping or not eating or . . . ?"

"No," I said. "What about your life has caused you the most sadness or anxiety or made you the angriest? What *hurt* you?"

"Nothing," she said immediately.

I waited.

She shrugged. "I don't know. . . . If I had to say something, I guess I'd say I didn't exactly love leaving Ohio as a kid. Does that count?"

"How old were you?"

"Eight."

When a person remembers emotional pain from more than a decade ago, it definitely counts. I told her so and asked her to tell me why she remembered that year as a difficult one.

"I had to leave my school and my friends," she said. "And I wasn't used to moving around yet."

"Why did you have to leave?" I asked.

"My dad divorced my mom," she said. She sighed and looked away.

"How many times have you moved since?" I asked.

She laughed but without joy. "I stopped counting at fifteen."

By the end of our session together, I had learned that Rachel's mother took her and her brothers to Los Angeles following the divorce. Her father didn't make any attempt to keep his children nearer to him. And when Los Angeles didn't seem to offer her mother a good enough job or a good enough relationship, she moved the family to San Diego. Then, every year or two, she moved them again, usually after breaking up with a man, as if one more change of scenery would finally change their lives.

There's a very wise saying: *Wherever you go, there you are.*

Geographic cures don't work. Running from her demons—from her pain—couldn't have healed Rachel's mother's underlying psychological injuries. And it had real potential to injure Rachel.

"She wasn't worried you would have trouble adjusting to so many moves?" I asked.

"I don't know," Rachel said. "I've never asked her what she was thinking."

There were other things Rachel and her mother had never spoken of, including the circumstances that had led to her parents' divorce, circumstances that could have shed light on why her father made little or no effort to stay in touch with her or her brothers.

The unexamined chapters of Rachel's life story were full of potential pain. It didn't surprise me that she felt as if she needed to use cocaine to keep that pain at bay. And it didn't surprise me in the least that cocaine had never done the trick.

I met with Rachel a few more times and helped her confront the things she had been trying to avoid. We talked about how many friends she had left behind over the course of so many moves. We talked about how much it really did hurt that her father hadn't done more to keep her close. And we talked about how angry she really was that her mother had forced her to pull up the meager roots she put down in city after city as a little girl.

Then I had her mother join us.

It was obvious to me that Wendy loved her daughter. I knew she was driving nearly three hours to bring her to see me. I knew she was sacrificing income she desperately needed. Her voice cracked as she described how Rachel had changed after she started using cocaine. She cried as she spoke about her fear that Rachel would kill herself.

There wasn't any chance that in meeting with Rachel and Wendy, I was simply with a victim and a perpetrator. I knew from listening to thousands of other stories that Wendy had to have been injured psychologically herself to be blind to the ways in which she had injured Rachel. "What was your dad like?" I asked her.

"Why does that matter right now?" Wendy asked.

"You and Rachel have never spoken about why her father doesn't stay in touch with her, or how she feels about that fact, so I'm guessing you have a reason not to go near the subject. Maybe it has something to do with *your* father."

Wendy shrugged in exactly the way Rachel had during our first meeting. "I didn't know my father very well, either. My parents split up while my mom was pregnant with me."

"Did you spend any real time with your dad?" I asked.

"No," she said immediately.

"Is that something that's caused you a lot of pain?"

"Not at all."

"Why wouldn't it?" I asked Wendy.

"My mother always told me she loved me enough for two parents," she said. "I never felt like I needed anyone else."

When a mother *tells* a daughter that her love should be enough to make up for the absence of that girl's father, she makes it very hard for the daughter to disagree. To do so would risk offending the only reliable support the girl has in the world. Yet Wendy never truly felt she had had all the love she needed. That's why, as an adult, she would find herself constantly moving from one state to another, running from broken relationships. Abandoned by her father, she craved male attention and took it extraordinarily hard when a man withdrew that affection. "Did your mom remarry?" I asked her.

"No," Wendy said.

"Was there anyone special that came into her life—and yours?"

"Where are you going with this?" Wendy asked.

People usually ask that question when I'm moving closer to their pain. "I just wondered whether your mother fell in love again and let that man get to know you."

"There was one person," she said, seemingly reluctantly. "Sam."

"Nice person?"

She was silent for a few moments. She cleared her throat. "Very."

"Was he kind to you?"

"To all of us," she said. "He was a wonderful man. Very generous. Very patient. A gentleman."

"And what happened to him?" I asked.

"I don't know. I mean, my mom stopped seeing him, and . . ." She shrugged. Her eyes filled up with tears. She fought them back, then took a deep breath. "And that was the end of that," she said.

But it wasn't the "end of that." It was only the beginning. Wendy lost contact with her father, then lost another father figure, and it had kept her running from rejection her whole life. And that had set the stage for her daughter to inherit the same toxic psychological dynamic.

I have no doubt that Wendy's mother—Rachel's grandmother—had her own issues with abandonment, hence her flawed decree that her love for Wendy should have been equivalent to the love of both a father and a mother.

Three generations of women had been fighting the same emotional demons. And I do not believe for a moment that those demons were encoded in their DNA. I believe they were passed, mother to daughter, because each woman feared her demons and fled them rather than face them. And that only made their demons stronger, until, in Rachel's life, they finally created conditions—major depression and cocaine dependence—that could not be ignored.

Rachel went in search of her father. When she found him, he did the right thing: he apologized to her. He admitted that his fear of fathering and of commitment led him to allow time and distance to come between them. And he swore that he would stay in her life from that day forward.

Once Rachel faced the sadness of having been separated from her father, once she confronted the resulting unconscious questions she harbored about whether she was lovable, she started to love herself. She got sober, she agreed to use an antidepressant temporarily, and her symptoms of depression remitted.

Three generations of women. Three generations spent, in part, running from the truth. And yet the singular resolve of one of those women to look squarely at her pain was ultimately more powerful than decades of denial.

It can be every bit as powerful in your life.

FACING THE TRUTH WITH FORGIVENESS

Identifying the ways in which you were injured as a child, adolescent, or young adult is by no means taking the easy way out or looking for an excuse to blame anyone for your suffering. It is simply accepting the reality that you were injured and refusing to bury that reality for yet another generation, thereby extinguishing its toxic potential in your own lifetime.

Of course, many of my patients do become angry as they realize that the actions of others have diminished their lives. But here again, religion intersects with psychiatry. Because to accept your pain, grow from it, and truly become greater than it ultimately requires forgiving others for inflicting it upon you. It requires realizing they did so out of ignorance and fear and the very same resistance to feeling and owning their own pain that you are now—*only now*—committed to overcoming.

The truth always wins, but it can take a long time. The fact that its moment may be at hand right now, with this book as a guide, is something to celebrate and build upon, not something to feel guilty about or to squander on perpetual rage.

Author Harry Crews (whom I first quoted in chapter three)

tells a story about his own childhood that I find instructive. When he was a young boy, he was playing pop-the-whip with his brother and cousins. Pop-the-whip is a game in which children join hands and run in a line. The first child turns suddenly, and that creates a kind of chain reaction with increasing force down the line, so that the last child is popped loose and sent flying.

Crews was the last child in the line. But when he popped loose, he tumbled into a steaming pot of water that was being used to cook a pig. When he stood up, much of his skin had literally melted.

And here's the miraculous and instructive memory about his mother and uncle that Crews puts to paper:

> Hands were on me, taking off my clothes, and the pain turned into something words cannot touch, or at least my words cannot touch. There is no way for me to talk about it because when my shirt was taken off, my back came off with it. When my overalls were pulled down, my cooked and glowing skin came down.
>
> I still had not fallen, and I stood there participating in my own butchering. When they got the clothes off me, they did the worst thing they could have done; they wrapped me in a sheet. They did it out of panic and terror and ignorance and love.

So many of our psychological injuries are like Harry Crews's burns and the horrific compounding of that damage his mother and uncle caused him when they wrapped him in a sheet (which meant that the sheet had to be peeled off Harry by a doctor, causing him even more pain and worse scarring). The people who inflict injuries upon us generally do so out of panic and terror and ignorance and, more than half the time, what they think of as love.

Take, for instance, the story of Erica and her parents. Erica was thirty-nine when she first came to see me. Her marriage to an alcoholic had recently ended, but not before her husband's erratic behavior had led to the loss of their home and to Erica having to file personal bankruptcy. "It's embarrassing enough by itself," she said, "but this is something no one in my family has ever had to deal with. My mother and father have been together forty-five years, and they're still happy. Nobody can believe this is happening."

"Tell me about your parents," I said. "What does your dad do for work?"

"He owns a stationery shop," she said. "He opened it a few years after he married my mom."

"Does she work there?" I asked.

"She did for a few years," Erica said.

"And then decided to stay home to take care of you?"

"I think so. I mean, I'm an only child. It would have been to take care of me, I guess."

Confusion so often precedes clarity. "How old were you?" I asked.

"I don't think I had been born yet," she said. "I don't think she would even have been pregnant when she stopped working."

Erica was thirty-nine and focusing for the first time on why her father had ended up running the family business alone. That meant that something in the story was emotionally threatening to her. I stayed silent to allow the truth a chance to fill the void.

"I remember my dad saying something about her moods at the time being out of control," Erica said finally. "He laughs about it now." She chuckled to herself. "My mom was giving stuff away one day and throwing people out of the store the next. I guess you could say she wasn't exactly helping the business."

"Were her moods predictable when you were growing up?" I asked.

She stopped smiling. "Not always," she said. "She wasn't out of control or anything, but she had her highs and lows."

"Did she ever see a psychiatrist?"

"I'm not sure. I think so."

"Did she take medicine?" I asked.

She shrugged. "Probably. I think I remember my dad bringing it home for her one time from the drugstore, and them arguing about whether she needed to take it." She smiled again. "She always said I was her best medicine."

It might seem extraordinary that Erica had never really focused on the precise reason her mother had stopped working or on the fact that her mother needed medicine to control her unwieldy moods and behavior. Erica had never asked her father why her mother would be extraordinarily generous at work one day and full of rage the next. But many of my patients have shown the same blind spots for painful parts of the past. And every one of those patients has reminded me of the mind's powerful capacity to deny reality and repress suffering.

It took only one more session for the truth to become crystal clear. Before that session, Erica had asked her father about her mother's condition and learned she had been diagnosed with bipolar disorder. She had been treated for it with lithium, but the medicine never worked well enough for her to return to work. And Erica, as an only child at home with her mom, really was a great comfort to her—her *best medicine*.

Never having examined what she had lived through as the daughter of a woman struggling with a psychiatric disorder, never having revisited what it had meant to love someone deeply and take care of someone who was supposed to be taking care of *her*, Erica never "outgrew" it. She remained locked in the dynamic that defined her childhood.

When it came time for Erica to marry, she found a situation that reproduced the one she had grown up with. She was the breadwinner; her husband was ill (with alcoholism) and needed her for stability. She felt as if she were his *best medicine*. She felt *at home* in a relationship that echoed the one she had had as a little girl at home with her bipolar mother. But while Erica's marriage reproduced the past faithfully in some respects, she had chosen a man even more fragile than her mother and someone who could not be trusted with the family finances. And she paid the price—not only with divorce but with personal bankruptcy.

For a time Erica grew angry at her mother. After all, she wondered aloud, wasn't it predictable that relying on a little girl to keep things together (rather than getting more professional help) would turn that girl into a caregiver for life?

Erica also grew angry at her father for letting her play such an adult role in childhood, which she correctly saw as fostering her codependency (with her husband) in adulthood.

"Why didn't he protect me?" she asked tearfully during one session with me. "Why didn't he see that she was using me and make her stop?"

Erica's anger was short-lived. Because once she resolved to seek the whole truth from her parents, she learned that her mother had suffered much more as a child than Erica ever knew. She had grown up with an extremely violent stepfather who beat her and humiliated her. And Erica's grandmother hadn't protected her daughter at all.

Erica also learned more about her father. She knew he had lost his own mother to cancer as a boy, but she had never spoken with him about it. And she learned he could still be brought to tears describing how helpless he felt watching the mother he adored waste away.

Knowing her parents' pain—their backstories—sparked Erica's empathy. She could understand why her mother's moods would have become erratic; as a little girl she had lived through countless days that seemed to promise a happy ending, only to fracture into unpredictable violence. And she could understand why her father, having felt so powerless to help his sick mother, would have chosen a woman who both needed and welcomed his help.

Rather than continuing to blame her parents for her suffering, Erica forgave them. Because she realized that they had never freed themselves from the pain of the past by doing the very thing she had finally done—facing it. Her parents were both limited in the kind of parenting they could give because they were running from what they had lived through long before she was born.

The ultimate toll of not looking at the past and facing your pain is that your free will and ability to care for others is eroded or erased. You can easily become the unwitting servant of blind spots in your psyche rather than a clear thinker who can protect the people you love.

STORIES OF FORGIVENESS

Sometimes it's easier to see how the past influences the present and determines the future when you see those forces operating in someone else's life. Write a story about how your parents' personalities and behavior patterns have been shaped by the experiences each lived through growing up. If you don't know the most powerful events and relationships they experienced as young people, ask them directly or ask people who knew them when they were young, using the advice about how to talk to your friends and family that was outlined in the previous chapter. You may well discover things about your parents you've never heard before. This is all about getting past your family fiction to the *truth* about your family. It's always facts that inspire empathy; only what is real can connect us to one another.

Stories you've learned about your mother:

_____

_____

_____

_____

_____

_____

_____

Stories you've learned about your father:

_____

_____

_____

_____

_____

_____

Next, think about what unresolved issues in your parents' life stories may have been unwittingly handed down to you. Ask yourself how your history of struggling to become genuine and powerful really goes back generations.

Have my mother's issues been handed down to me? If so, how?

_____

_____

_____

_____

_____

_____

_____

_____

_____

Have my father's issues been handed down to me? If so, how?

_____

_____

_____

_____

_____

_____

_____

_____

The following exercises may help you better understand the reasons your parents were unable to keep their psychological injuries from becoming yours. This doesn't excuse their behavior, but it may explain it, thereby making you resent it less. Feel free to call your parents or visit them, and ask them to help you fill in the blanks.

The toughest challenges my mother faced in becoming a complete and loving person were:
(*Example: "The toughest challenges my mother faced in becoming a complete and loving person were* her learning disability and resulting low grades, which made everyone around her think she was unintelligent for so many years. That set her up to be valued only for her looks, and she never developed real self-esteem.")

_____

_____

_____

_____

_____

The toughest challenges my father faced in becoming a complete and loving person were:
(*Example: "The toughest challenges my father faced in becoming a complete and loving person were* his own mother's neglect and the way she set him up to need so much attention and reassurance from the women in his life.")

_____

_____

_____

_____

_____

If I could have magically spared my parents pain from their past, I would have rewritten their life histories without the following events:

(Example: "If I could have magically spared my parents pain from their past, I would have rewritten their life histories with-out the following events: the loss of my paternal grandfather to heart disease when my father was eleven, and the senseless argument that ended my mother's relationship with her sister. I don't think my dad ever felt secure again, and expressed that by trying to control everything and everyone around him. And I think my mother put up with it to avoid the kind of blowup she'd had with my aunt.")

_____

_____

_____

_____

_____

_____

While my mother was far from perfect, she improved on the kind of parenting she experienced as a girl in this way:

(Example: "While my mother was far from perfect, she improved on the kind of parenting she experienced as a girl in this way: she still had a bad habit of yelling like everyone in her family, but un-like her own mother, she never hit me.")

_____

_____

_____

_____

_____

_____

While my father was far from perfect, he improved on the kind of parenting he experienced as a boy in this way:
(*Example:* "*While my father was far from perfect, he improved on the kind of parenting he experienced as a boy in this way:* my father's own parents didn't go to college, and neither did he. And even though he was relentlessly critical of my decision to pursue a career in music, he did work his heart out to make sure I could go to college, even when I switched my concentration from engineering to music studies.")

_____

_____

_____

_____

_____

You may not be able to fill in every blank. Maybe your parents aren't in touch with their own pain enough to give you insights into the challenges that limited their personal development. Or maybe you can't think of any way your father did better as a parent than his own father did for him. If you're lucky enough to have living parents, you may want to lend them a copy of *Living the Truth* to get them started on their own paths of self-discovery. If they take even a few steps, that can only help you on your own journey to the truth.

• • •

Living the truth means feeling the pain of the past; forgiving those who unwittingly, blindly inflicted it upon us; and resolving to do better for ourselves and those we love. This is the highest form of human existence. And it is within reach for anyone with the courage and determination to dig deep, even in darkness, to find the buried treasure that is the just reward of an examined life.

PART THREE
LIVING THE
TRUTH NOW

CHAPTER 10

Getting to Your True Desire

Imagine if you were asked to read several chapters of a novel beginning on page 117, ignoring the first 116 pages, and then to write the last five chapters of the story, including a compelling ending true to the main character's heart and soul.

The assignment would test the confidence of any writer, make him or her feel anxious and frustrated, and quite possibly make the writer bow out of the exercise altogether. The person might well feel like a fraud, as though he or she didn't really *know* the character involved—and not merely where that character was from or what he had done, but what made him *tick*.

The writer would be missing what storytellers call the main character's *backstory,* all the relevant and dramatic conflicts he had faced earlier in life that had shaped his personality, relationships, and behaviors.

"This wasn't my story to begin with," the writer might think. "How am I supposed to know what should come next?"

Writing anything, never mind chapters designed to resolve

core difficulties in the main character's life, would be all but impossible.

Sound familiar?

Too many of us live our own lives in that manner—as authors of our own life stories, with the same nearly impossible task before us. We even use language that flows naturally from not "owning" our life stories. "I need to *find* myself." "I feel *lost.*" "I *can't believe* this is actually my life." "I feel like this is happening to *someone else.*"

Throughout this book, you have seen examples of people who are diminished in precisely this way. Denial and repression render them disempowered authors of their own existences. You have also seen by their examples that when they have confronted their suffering and recognized it for what it really is, they are empowered by it, not weakened by it.

If you have answered the questions and done the exercises in the first two sections of this book, you are well on your way to your own empowerment. In these final chapters, you will learn even more, including how to use everything you've discovered about yourself to get to your own true desires.

THE MORE DIFFICULT THE QUEST, THE GREATER THE REWARD

To fulfill almost any personal goal or desire, your focus has to be on what it is about yourself that could be getting in your way. This is true in sports, academics, and the arts, and it is no less true in romance, dieting, overcoming an addiction, or achieving any aspect of your life plan. Great architects don't become great by spending time celebrating how exceptional they are at mechanical drawing or the use of unique building materials while ignoring other important skills they need to do their job. They become great by challenging themselves to reach the same level of excellence in the use of space and light (or in any other aspects of their craft). It wouldn't do to spend a lot of time taking pride in your lung capacity while the vessels of your heart are clogged. And it won't do to use career success to blind yourself to trouble in your relationships.

Becoming healthy psychologically is no different from getting healthy physically. It is about identifying weaknesses and then overcoming them.

The best question to ask yourself in order to grow into the person you want to be is, what would you *change* about yourself or your existence right now if you had the chance? What exactly *isn't* working well? What would make you admire yourself more? What would make you a better person? What would make you a better example to your children, or their children? Would you break free of a relationship that's limiting you or eroding your self-esteem? Would you find the courage to finally commit to one man or one woman and raise a family? Would you take the chance to leave a job that doesn't fulfill you? Would you stop overspending and start investing wisely? Would you worry less about the future and live more in the moment? Would you lose weight and get fit?

The moment you identify trouble in your life, you've identified a goal—finding the truth behind that trouble (exactly what in your life story made you vulnerable to it) and turning it into your treasure.

Getting to your true desire really is that straightforward. It is a three-step process:

1. Identify the trouble spots that need the most attention.

Why do you need to specify which of your trouble spots need immediate attention? Because although most of us pride ourselves on our ability to multitask, when it comes to "fixing" what's wrong with our lives, it's best to concentrate on one thing at a time. Often, solving one problem automatically eliminates others. Suppose you are a compulsive overeater. You are overweight, you have diabetes, your knees hurt, and you can't walk up a flight of stairs without losing your breath. You can choose to concentrate on eliminating the pain in your knees and spend time and money pursuing a cure. However, if you were to focus instead on the issue of compulsive eating, discover the cause behind it, and develop a plan to lose weight, your related health issues would likely disappear on their own.

2. Embrace the truth behind your trouble spots.

Why is it so important to embrace the truth behind your trouble? Because nothing in the universe stays fixed for very long if the underlying *cause* isn't known, accepted, and addressed. In an abusive relationship, for instance, you can get rid of a man who's been eroding your self-esteem, but you will have treated only a symptom of the problem. When you figure out why you included a man like that in your life, you've uncovered the underlying *cause* of the problem. And that means you have a chance to avoid other abusive men in the future. Going back to an analogy from the body, you can clear a cardiac artery of plaque, but if the problem is high cholesterol, the artery will clog again eventually. If you treat a fever but not the underlying infection, you risk letting that infection do more and more damage.

3. Devise a plan to turn your personal truth into your personal treasure.

Why is a plan critical? Because plans help you tolerate the inevitable pain on your way to power. Taking the analogy to physical improvement one step further, if you know that physical therapy will help you get your strength and balance back after years of favoring one limb over another, you can grit your teeth and bear it a whole lot better. You can hold yourself to specific standards in moving toward your goal. And you can document your progress. It's no different with improving your emotional balance. When you start to refuse the money that comes from a well-paying job that is keeping you from your true life's work, it can hurt at first. Not only are you deprived of the toys you once used to distract yourself but you are confronted with new questions about whether you'll meet with success in pursuing what you love. Taking that risk demands courage, and having a realistic vision of the hurdles in your way, the timeline required to achieve your objectives, and the rewards that would satisfy you will help you stay the course.

Step One: Identifying the Trouble Spots in Your Life

You already know what's troubling you. You've written your life story and have probably identified several areas you feel need attention. For the moment, however, you're going to zero in on the specific areas that hold the most promise for dramatic change. Answering the questions below will help you do that.

- *What are you ambivalent about?*

When you are living your truth, you may experience mild self-doubt, but feeling substantially unsettled about anything in your existence is a clue that what is upsetting you may mean real trouble ahead. Do you drive to work and stop for coffee twice because you need to do something pleasant on your way to a workday you actually find distasteful? Do you hesitate to introduce your romantic partner to your friends because, deep inside, you know they'll see he or she isn't good for you? Do you pretty much have to convince yourself that your father is a reliable enough person to allow to spend the day with your children? Do you scrimp and save compulsively when you actually have enough money to spend more on the things you love to do?

List three things about which you are ambivalent:

1. _____

2. _____

3. _____

I'm most *ambivalent about:*

_____

- *What are you secretive about?*

With rare exception, human beings attempt to hide their real troubles not only from themselves but from others. We are easily shamed and worry that we will be ostracized for our foibles. If only we can cover up, we can keep our family, friends, and romantic partners close.

Of course, the opposite is true. No relationship is real (or close) if it isn't based on the other person really knowing you. But it doesn't *feel* that way to most people.

How about you? What do you try to hide from others? An eating problem? A gambling addiction? Your mother's unwieldy, embarrassing moods? The fact that you had too little money growing up? The fact that you were bullied in school or had learning problems? The fact that you don't think you're the kind of mother you always wanted to be?

This is *your* book, no one else's. It's time to stop keeping secrets—at least from yourself.

List three things you are secretive about:

1. _____

2. _____

3. _____

I'm most *secretive about:*

_____

- *What are you embarrassed by?*

Being embarrassed by the behavior of a member of your family, the job you hold, the man you're dating, your body, your eating, the way you allow yourself to be manipulated, the lack of control you have over a child, the fact that you are rageful toward a child, your educational background, or anything else about your life is a dramatic sign that you can find personal treasure by thinking more about it.

Embarrassment is the sense that a problem is bigger than you and unique to you. You can't control it, and others won't understand it or condone it. But that isn't true. Perhaps it was true when you were a child, or before you resolved to take control of your existence, but it isn't now. So you need to look at what you are embarrassed about and resolve to find out why.

List three things you are embarrassed by or about:

1. _____

2. _____

3. _____

I'm most *embarrassed by or about:*

_____

- *What do you dread?*

Buried in your fear is your freedom. What you dread in life is probably a close cousin of something you have lived through already, or at least something you worried about from a very early age. Do you dread giving up any control to anyone? Do you dread that you'll hear you've suddenly lost someone you love? Do you dread having your intellect or appearance judged harshly? Or is your deepest fear one of being rejected by the person or the people you live with?

To find the truth behind your trouble, you need to begin seeing these fears as clues, then backtracking to find their roots in your early life experiences. The fear of losing someone you love, for example, is often fueled by never having dealt with the loss of a loved one in childhood. But it can also be fueled by never having been confident that your parents would really stay together or stick by your side.

List three of your greatest fears:

1. _____

2. _____

3. _____

My greatest *fear is:*

_____

- *What can't you stomach when you see it in others?*

As adults, the behaviors and personality traits that bother us most in others may be ones that we once *had to* live with as younger people. A controlling person, or a person who is quick to judge others, or a person who lets herself be overpowered by the men in her life, or a person who drinks to excess, or a person who is unethical in business may be unattractive to most. But if you find your blood boiling when you so much as think of a particular individual, it might be because he or she reminds you of someone else you've had to deal with—someone who left you with unwieldy, unresolved feelings.

Three behaviors or personality traits that bother me when I observe them in others are:

1. _____

2. _____

3. _____

The behavior or personality trait that bothers me the most is:

_____

- *What are the worst relationships you've ever been in (whether friendships or romances)?*

You never believed it could happen to you, right? You end up with someone who uses you or cheats on you repeatedly or lies compulsively or is an addict. And it took you a good long while to figure it out. And you still end up thinking about him or her from time to time, wondering why you can't forget the whole relationship, because you'd really like to.

As you now know, that relationship wasn't an accident. You were drawn to the person who disappointed you because something about him or her was very similar to a trait of someone you were close to growing up. And it felt like true love when you saw it because you convinced yourself it was part of being loved years and years ago.

My three worst relationships since leaving my childhood home have been:

1. _____

2. _____

3. _____

My absolute worst *relationship was:*

_____

- *What are the worst conflicts you've ever had on the job?*

The workplace is an environment that is likely to re-create dramas from our earlier life experience because it has elements in common with family life. People often spend many hours a day together. Rivalries and jealousies develop. And over time, it's tough for people to stay perfectly composed; they become more completely human.

The worst conflicts you've ever had in the workplace are likely to have been with people who remind you very much of others you struggled with in childhood. You probably haven't made the connection, but that's the work that will be done in step two. For now, just take several minutes to think back to the most dramatic interpersonal problems you've encountered on the job. A boss who took credit for all your hard work? A coworker who was constantly putting you down? Trouble containing your romantic feelings for a supervisor? Feeling paralyzed with paranoia that you were about to be fired (when you weren't)?

The three worst conflicts I've encountered on the job have been:

1. _____

2. _____

3. _____

The worst *conflict I've encountered on the job has been:*

_____

- *What kind of situation makes you want to give up rather than fight?*

The set of circumstances or kind of person that takes all the wind out of your sails is often the one that hearkens back most directly to childhood. That's why you may believe you have no more power in the situation than you did as a much younger individual. Of course, as an adult, you have many more resources. But that doesn't mean it *feels* that way. So what is it that makes you want to give up? Having your feelings completely disregarded, as if you don't matter? Being accused of something you're not guilty of? Being asked to share credit for something you did all by yourself? Being bullied by someone? Feeling that someone is withholding love from you?

Think of up to three situations that drain your willpower or leave you feeling completely vulnerable.

I feel like giving up completely when:

1. _____

2. _____

3. _____

The situation that most *makes me want to give up is:*

_____

- *What kind of situation makes you go overboard defending yourself?*

Just as the extreme of giving up in a certain situation or when confronting a particular kind of person can be a signpost on your way to the truth, so can the extreme of overreacting. Do you "go to war" whenever you think someone's questioning your intelligence? Do you "go for the jugular" when someone simply feels like spending time with someone other than you on a vacation? Do you "fight tooth and nail" whenever someone criticizes any family member of yours, even mildly? Do you "get your back up" in a hurry whenever someone in a position of authority leans on you a little?

A balanced response to conflict means that no underlying unconscious conflict has taken control. An overwhelmingly aggressive response to conflict means that you're really responding, at least in part, to leftover, unresolved life stories from the past.

The three times I remember going way overboard defending myself were:

1. _____

2. _____

3. _____

The one time I went the farthest *overboard was:*

_____

The lists you've just generated reflect some of the trouble spots you're encountering because of unresolved unconscious conflicts from the past. Look over your list of *most, worst,* etc., responses. I call these your "Life Story Clues," because once you realize what they are, they can help you solve the mystery of why you behave the way you do.

Below, list the nine Life Story Clues you filled in previously (e.g., I'm *most* ambivalent about . . . I'm *most* secretive about . . .).

My Life Story Clues:
1. *I'm* most *ambivalent about:*

_____

_____

_____

2. *I'm* most *secretive about:*

_____

_____

_____

3. *I'm* most *embarrassed by* or *about:*

_____

_____

_____

4. *My* greatest *fear is:*

_____

_____

_____

5. *The behavior or personality trait that bothers me the* most *is:*

_____

_____

_____

6. *My absolute* worst *relationship was:*

_____

_____

_____

7. *The* worst *conflict I've encountered on the job has been:*

_____

_____

_____

8. *The situation that* most *makes me want to give up is:*

_____

_____

_____

9. *The one time I went the* farthest *overboard was:*

_____

_____

_____

Now it's time to stop running, to look directly at the truth behind these Life Story Clues and unlock your personal treasure—what you truly desire.

Step Two: Embrace the Truth Behind Your Trouble Spots

The human soul is like a divining rod that points to the truth. Pay attention, and you'll be drawn naturally in the right direction. Paying attention is easier said than done, however, because the mind has an opposite and unfortunate tendency to distract you from any truth that is painful.

For every Life Story Clue you listed, there's a real reason *why* you've encountered that pain or stress. It's fallout from an unresolved conflict or disappointment earlier in your life. And it's time to put in the effort to look squarely at each one of them.

If you're ambivalent about going to work, it's time to sit down and write out exactly what about your work is scary or unsatisfying. But don't stop there. Become an investigator of your own dissatisfaction. Wonder why, given your previous painful life experiences, that aspect of your work would frighten you. Why would you spend so many of your days pursuing something that doesn't speak to your soul? Did you have a goal in mind as a young person that your parents didn't support? Did that hurt so much that you lost faith you could ever achieve what was actually in your heart to accomplish?

If you dread giving up control over any aspect of your life (even weekend plans), now's the time to figure out *why*. When in your life were you *overly controlled* and by whom?

If you find yourself in a romantic relationship where you're constantly criticized yet can't seem to break free, now is the time to wonder what in your upbringing made you so desperate for approval from a withholding person that you can't leave him (or her). Are you replaying a drama that you experienced with your father or mother—depending on a person who withholds unconditional love?

Or take the opposite extreme: you can't stand being criticized at all, about anything. There's a reason *why*: your early experiences with criticism. So what were they? Were you overly indulged as a child, prevented from learning that love can coexist with honest and well-meaning reviews of your performance? Or was every bit of criticism you received contaminated by anger and manipulation that hinted you were not well enough regarded by a teacher or a coach, or well enough loved by a parent?

If you "go to war" when someone accuses you of being selfish, maybe even having ended a friendship over a single comment, then the theme of selfishness was almost certainly a dramatic and painful one in your childhood. Were you always the giving child, always the one taken advantage of by your siblings? Is that why you're now enraged when anyone suggests you would put yourself first? Now's the time to embrace the connection between what is not working in your life at present and the painful truths of your life in the past. When you start to think about your trouble spots, you may feel bad about yourself for being needy, or selfish, or controlling, or for being somehow "broken" or flawed. But those bad feelings are actually your friends. Because they're reliable clues to how to change your life for the better.

The most dramatic problems in your life today are mere reflections of difficulties you encountered many years ago but never dealt with head-on. That's why you find yourself mystified as to why the trouble keeps cropping up. Now you've begun to make the connection between past and present.

And the key tool in this exploration of the past is having ultimate respect for that simple one-word question—*Why?* Commit right now to answering the "why" question for each of the situations you listed above. Your response must be about what you experienced during your first two decades of life (and probably your first fifteen years) that set the stage for your emotions or behavior today.

Focus particularly on these potential sources of pain: early losses, rivalries, jealousies, disappointments (with others or yourself), and trauma.

For each Life Story Clue on pages 213–214, write the word "because" beside it. Then answer the "why" question by creating a sensible and persuasive sentence that ties today's troubles to yesterday's truths.

Here are some examples:

"*My absolute* worst *relationship was* with a man who criticized me all the time about my weight *because* my father used to do the same thing. That made me wonder how anyone could do that to someone he loved."

"*I'm* most *secretive about* my acting lessons *because* my mother always said trying to be an actress was ridiculous."

"*The one time I went the* farthest *overboard was* when my friend accused me of flirting with her boyfriend *because* my sister had a bad habit of stealing the guys I dated in high school, and I pride myself on being a lot more trustworthy than she was."

"*The situation that* most *makes me want to give up is* when anyone I love gets really sick and needs my help *because* I lost my dad when I was thirteen and couldn't do anything to help him."

"*The* worst *conflict I've ever encountered on the job has been* when my boss didn't give me credit for an idea he presented at a conference *because* I looked at him as a father figure, and he let me down (just like my father always did)."

"*The behavior or personality trait that bothers me the* most *is* being cheap *because* I had so little growing up that I now take real pleasure in not scrimping or saving."

Using the word "because" to turn your Life Story Clues into truthful sentences about your past pain is hard work. In some ways, it's the work of a lifetime compressed into *these* particular moments. Dedicate yourself to the task, honor the divining rod in your soul that desperately wants you to find your truth, and you can save yourself a lifetime of running from it. Every sentence you write from your heart is a precious key to your treasure chest of self-possession.

Step Three: Devising a Plan to Turn Your Personal Truth into Your Personal Treasure

Each sentence you've completed in the way I've indicated is a very clear sign of what matters to you in life. Each contains a trouble spot and its roots in the past. And each, therefore, points in a direction you need to grow for you to find peace, pleasure, and fulfillment.

How? By putting your fear and disappointment back where they belong—in the past. Let yourself feel the pain you've been avoiding, and you will become powerful in equal measure.

Take this example.

"*My absolute* worst *relationship was* with a man who criticized me all the time about my weight *because* my father used to do the same thing. That made me wonder how anyone could do that to someone he loved."

How do you turn this past pain into a plan for future contentment? There are several steps you can take:

• Sit down quietly and think of all those times your dad hurt you or embarrassed you by commenting on your weight. Let yourself feel as much of the sadness and betrayal of the past as humanly possible.

- Look at some photos of yourself as a child and wonder how anyone could have been unkind to you when you needed understanding.

- Have the courage to let yourself off the hook for your father's failings: you didn't disappoint him as a girl by not being fit. He let you down by not being a good enough father.

- Go back to what you learned from your father or from others who knew him about his own childhood experiences. Let yourself contemplate whether that means he was too damaged a man to offer you the unconditional love you needed as a child. Allow yourself to get angry, then practice the forgiveness exercise in chapter nine.

- Resolve to confront or remove from your life any man who is tethered to you by the same dynamic that tethered you to your father—constant criticism. Either he changes or you change partners.

- Have the courage to go find the man you really need. If you're going online to do it and your weight is still a sensitive issue, make sure you screen out anyone put off by a few extra pounds. On a date, be up front about who you are and what you need: "If you're looking for somebody skinny, that's not me."

Here's another example:

"*I'm* most *secretive about* my acting lessons *because* my mother always said trying to be an actress was ridiculous."

Think about what that means. Your mother didn't embrace your dreams. Will she now? Why not test the waters? Take the chance to tell her about your lessons. Maybe she'll surprise you and do better safeguarding your soul than she did when you were a child. Maybe that can be a crack in the wall of silence that's kept the two of you from being closer. Or maybe she'll disappoint you again, and you can finally tell her how it hurt you to have her doubt your talents. Maybe you'll even take the chance of inviting her to watch one of your lessons.

There's another possibility: your mother does no better this time than the last time. If that's the case, you might finally realize that she's the one with the problem, that there's no reason to hide your lessons from your true friends, because your mother was, sadly, never really one of them.

You might decide that the female acting teacher you've had can actually be more than that: a mentor. Maybe you'll take her to dinner and tell her how important she's become in your life. Maybe she'll play even more of a role in your personal development.

And here's the most important part: maybe you'll realize there's no reason to hide who you are from yourself any longer. You're an actor, and you're the child of a woman who couldn't embrace your dream (maybe because she never pursued her own). Maybe that's the pain to conjure up whenever you need to be in character and feeling betrayed.

Maybe you'll finally believe what your mother never did: that now is the moment to commit to acting half-time or even full-time. Or maybe you're ready to get an agent. Just make sure you really take the opportunity to stretch: find a female agent about your mom's age.

One more example:

"The situation that most *makes me want to give up is* when anyone I love gets really sick and needs my help *because* I lost my dad when I was thirteen and couldn't do anything to help him."

How to turn that trouble into triumph? Think back to being thirteen. How did you first hear your dad was ill? Where were you? Who told you? How did you feel? Who did you call? When did you first know he was starting to lose his strength?

Tough questions. It'll hurt to answer them. That's the idea. Put the pain back where it belongs—in the past. Then turn it into power.

What if you started to wonder why you've avoided asking your sister about her health problems, calling her up, hearing what she's been suffering from, and becoming closer to her than ever? Maybe the two of you will realize you've never talked about losing your father and that it's high time you did.

Maybe you'll even remember that at eleven you dreamed of being a nurse or a doctor, but abandoned that life plan when your dad died in the hospital. Maybe you'll decide it isn't too late to rekindle that dream and pursue it.

Or maybe you'll notice that you always do something to ruin relationships when they take a turn toward love because the first man you ever cared for—your dad—left you. Maybe you'll understand that you'll miss him forever, but that you're missing out on something he would have wanted for you: a relationship and a family. Maybe you'll finally see that his memory is best honored by taking the risk of losing someone you love—again, not running away from it.

Every person is a story. And your story is held hostage to the past to the extent that you *run* from the pain of the past. Turn around, face it, and run straight toward it, and you will find the next and most powerful chapters of your life.

Here's how to start right now. Below, transcribe each of the Life Story Clues you've created, then add this half sentence and complete it:

Therefore, if I'm really going to show courage and use my pain to become more powerful and move in the direction of my true desires, I'm going to take the chance to:

Here's an example:

"*My absolute* worst *relationship was* with a man who criticized me all the time about my weight *because* my father used to do the same thing. That made me wonder how anyone could do that to someone he loved. *Therefore, if I'm really going to show courage and use my pain to become more powerful and move in the direction of my true desires, I'm going to take the chance to* stop avoiding situations in which I might be criticized. And when a friend or romantic partner is critical of me, I'm going to ask him or her to explain more about his or her feelings, instead of running away from the situation."

Complete your Life Story Clues here:
1. *I'm* most *ambivalent about:*

_____

_____

_____

Therefore, if I'm really going to show courage and use my pain to become more powerful and move in the direction of my true desires, I'm going to take the chance to:

_____

_____

_____

2. *I'm* most *secretive about:*

_____

_____

_____

Therefore, if I'm really going to show courage and use my pain to become more powerful and move in the direction of my true desires, I'm going to take the chance to:

_____

_____

_____

3. *I'm* most *embarrassed by or about:*

_____

_____

_____

Therefore, if I'm really going to show courage and use my pain to become more powerful and move in the direction of my true desires, I'm going to take the chance to:

_____

_____

_____

4. *My* greatest *fear is:*

_____

_____

_____

Therefore, if I'm really going to show courage and use my pain to become more powerful and move in the direction of my true desires, I'm going to take the chance to:

_____

_____

_____

5. *The behavior or personality trait that bothers me the* most *is:*

_____

_____

_____

Therefore, if I'm really going to show courage and use my pain to become more powerful and move in the direction of my true desires, I'm going to take the chance to:

_____

_____

_____

6. *My absolute* worst *relationship was:*

_____

_____

_____

Therefore, if I'm really going to show courage and use my pain to become more powerful and move in the direction of my true desires, I'm going to take the chance to:

_____

_____

_____

7. *The* worst *conflict I've encountered on the job has been:*

_____

_____

_____

Therefore, if I'm really going to show courage and use my pain to become more powerful and move in the direction of my true desires, I'm going to take the chance to:

_____

_____

_____

8. *The situation that* most *makes me want to give up is:*

_____

_____

_____

Therefore, if I'm really going to show courage and use my pain to become more powerful and move in the direction of my true desires, I'm going to take the chance to:

_____

_____

_____

9. *The one time I went the* farthest *overboard was:*

_____

_____

_____

Therefore, if I'm really going to show courage and use my pain to become more powerful and move in the direction of my true desires, I'm going to take the chance to:

_____

_____

_____

These are your sentences to complete. And the only thing in your way is fear. I know you can overcome it. I know you can do more than survive the troubles you've turned away from. I know you can look squarely at them, live the truth, and find out that you love yourself more than you ever knew. And from that moment on, the sky is truly the limit.

CHAPTER 11

Envisioning the Future

Every great story has an arc. The lead character begins with all sorts of weaknesses, fears, and foibles and, by confronting adversity, finally faces the truth about his or her existence. The person's deep character is revealed. No longer is that individual's future destined to be merely an echo of one childhood drama or another, a never-ending replay of the past. A heroic journey of personal discovery has been undertaken and completed.

Rarely do we embrace a story in which the main character fails to rise to the occasion. Imagine Rocky Balboa deciding he doesn't really want a title shot because his dad always told him he would be a failure. Imagine Paul Newman's character in *The Verdict* deciding he might as well settle his malpractice case with the archdiocese quickly so he can keep drinking. Imagine Norma Rae deciding her self-esteem really wasn't sufficient to confront a powerful company.

Even superheroes take their power from their pain. Superman wouldn't be Superman were it not for the fact that he was orphaned and sent to another planet as an infant. Batman wouldn't be Batman were it not for the murder of his parents and his phobia about bats.

You may already know what would give you the sense of "wholeness" you are seeking. Hopefully, having completed the exercises in the previous chapter, you are closer than ever to identifying some of the issues you need to resolve to get there.

YOU ARE THE HERO OF YOUR OWN LIFE STORY

Now I want to help you see straight through to a future with your buried treasure in hand and your dearest goals either attained or within reach. That will make you able to see yourself as the hero of your own life story. And seeing that magnificent personal evolution can be critical to making it your reality. Here are some steps you can take to help you see yourself in this very different light:

- *Keep the very last step at the front of your mind.*

None of us will live forever. Our life stories will end. Trying to deny that fact makes it very difficult to summon the will to implement major changes sooner rather than later. The truth is that when you focus on who you want to be when saying good-bye to this world and imagine yourself the most complete and satisfied person possible, you will enrich every step of your journey.

- *Imagine what you would want someone you love very much to be able to say about your personal evolution.*

Perhaps it's your spouse, your parents, your sister or brother, your son or daughter, or your very best friend. Imagine that person delivering a moving account of where you were at this moment in life and the ways in which you were able to change before your life ended.

I know this isn't an easy task. It's one you'll be tempted to avoid. Your mind will veer away from the sadness of thinking about your epitaph. But it's sadder to think about not being fully alive while you have the chance. So take yourself in hand and approach this head-on.

What story of your personal evolution would make your loved one most proud? That you ended an addiction to alcohol? That you overcame low self-esteem and went back to school for an advanced degree? That you quit a lucrative job that meant nothing to you in order to take one that paid less but spoke to your soul? Would you want your husband or wife to say you committed yourself to rekindling romance in your marriage, that you decided to start a career after raising your kids, that you learned to stand up for yourself rather than always catering to others? Would you want him or her to be able to say you looked critically at your religion and selected one more closely aligned with your personal truth, that you finally stopped hiding your own history of abuse and started working with other victims, that you admitted depression or anxiety had always limited you and that you began psychotherapy (and maybe started taking an effective medicine)?

Think of the words you would most like to hear spoken about your journey through life. Write them down. Then take a single step toward living them — now.

What would you like your loved one(s) to say about you?

_____

_____

_____

_____

_____

- *Imagine what you would hope for the person you care about most in the world, if he or she were in your position.*

Sometimes it's easier to make courageous choices for the sake of others. Some women who can't summon the resolve to end their own abusive relationships would risk their lives to extract their daughters from them. Some men who have never dealt with their own low self-esteem would do anything in their power to help their sons conquer theirs. Many parents would buy their children memberships to a gym if their kids were out of shape but wouldn't do the same for themselves because it's "too expensive" or isn't "convenient."

What advice would you give the person you treasure most in life if that person were in your position? Hold that person in your mind and literally imagine your life story superimposed on the extraordinary concern you have for him or her. What changes would you urge him or her to make? How would you convince that individual to take the chance?

Linking the power of your love for another human being with your own journey can make it easier to begin. Why? Because you're actually harnessing the miraculous power of empathy, then reflecting the power back on yourself. The incredible human potential to feel for others (and help them do what they need to) is sometimes more powerful than our capacity to feel for ourselves (and do right by ourselves). So take a step outside yourself, look at yourself with the loving eyes you reserve for the person in the world for whom you would do anything, then do it for yourself.

Write down your hopes for yourself as though you were writing to a dear friend in your circumstances. Start with "I hope that you . . ."

_____

_____

_____

_____

_____

_____

_____

• *Don't be afraid to see your personal growth as an epic battle you must fight on all fronts.*

Make no mistake about it: embracing your truth and becoming the person you were meant to be is a war. You should be in a fighting mood. Not only are you opposing your own instinct to avoid psychological pain but you are opposing the instincts of others who may well discourage your exploration, especially if it puts them in touch with their own truths. And you are opposing the culture we live in that offers you every imaginable way to remain *out of touch* with your pain and your truth and be much less than you could be.

It may be in the narrow interests of your parents or your spouse or your friends to preserve the status quo and tell you it's silly to be reevaluating your life, and that you should just be happy with the way things are. But it isn't in your best i nterest.

It may be in the interest of insurance companies and some psychiatrists to quickly prescribe medicine when you feel anxious or depressed about life, but it is in your interest to make sure that if you take that medicine (which, in some circumstances, is a very good idea), it is coupled with a deep exploration of who you are and where your buried treasures of self-esteem and self-possession are to be found.

Becoming the complete, confident, self-actualized person you deserve to be doesn't mean just finding yourself; it means winning yourself back from forces aligned to keep your buried treasures of pain, desire, and potential hidden from you.

You can defeat them all handily. Because nothing in the world is more powerful than the truth. Keep moving with courage toward yours, and ultimately nothing will be able to stand in your way.

- *Write your own success story.*

Now is the time to decide what course of action would begin to make your story a triumphant one.

Ask yourself this question: if you were watching a movie in which the main character had your life story and was confronting the specific problems you've identified, what kinds of growth in that character would make you leave the theater smiling?

If you're a woman who had an untrustworthy father, that growth might be taking the risk to be truly honest and intimate with a man for the first time.

If you're a man whose older brother tormented you, it might be finally summoning the courage to ask for a male role model in business to be your mentor.

If you're someone who could never rely on parents to respond to your fears with support, then making one call to a lover to reveal a current anxiety about your work might change your way of being forever.

Success stories don't have to be sweeping. Taking small steps to free oneself from the psychological tethers of the past sets the stage for bigger steps down the road. Maybe your first step is to call a university to find out how to enroll as a part-time student, or to contact a therapist to make your first appointment, or to notify your boss that you're moving on, or to tell a dear friend you need to divulge something about your past, or to let your father know that the next time you see him you want to discuss the way his drinking embarrassed you as a girl—and continues to do so.

One step. But do it right now. Literally. Pick up the phone. Write a letter and mail it. Go online to find the detox center or NA meeting that's right for you, or the marriage counselor, or the fitness trainer, or the dating site, or the job-placement counselor. Just remember this: keep your final steps in mind, the personal goal you cherish, the life story you want your loved one to be able to tell about you.

You can learn that your adult world is not a replica of the world you inhabited as a child, that you can take emotional risks now that would have been too perilous back then—and often with spectacular results.

Now it's time to give yourself the chance to imagine what your life can be like if you take the steps you outlined previously. Think six months in the future, and write out what you see for yourself once you have confronted one or more trouble spots and transformed a romantic relationship, your body, your career, your performance as a parent, or whatever you value most highly:

_____

_____

_____

_____

_____

_____

Write down three specific steps you can take right now to demonstrate you are growing beyond the toxic lessons you learned as a child (e.g., you can call a therapist for an appointment, connect with your sister whom you haven't seen in years, enroll in a class or workshop, etc.).

1. _____

_____

2. _____

_____

3. _____

_____

Consider each of the steps above. Expand each one into a story about what you would be like if you were to take this step—how your life might change.

(*Example:* "I realize that I never trusted my sister, because my mother always pitted us against each other. If I apologize to her, I can have much richer friendships with women and stop relying on men to fulfill all my needs. Then maybe I can have a balanced relationship and actually find one man who wants to have an equal partnership. That might even lead to marriage and children.")

My step 1 story:

_____

_____

_____

_____

_____

_____

My step 2 story:

_____

_____

_____

_____

_____

_____

My step 3 story:

_____

_____

_____

_____

_____

_____

BECOMING THE HERO OF ONE STORY LINE
CAN HELP REWRITE OTHERS

The stakes of finding your true desire and living your truth could not be higher. Your own contentment hangs in the balance, but so, too, does the contribution and commitment you can offer to others, including your family, your friends, and your community.

I worked with a man whose story proves this point. Dennis was a thirty-four-year-old high-profile attorney. But he had become an attorney only because his parents had pressured him to give up his real dream of becoming an architect. They were intrusive people who had also persuaded him to marry someone of his own faith, when the only woman he had ever really loved was of another religion. Now he was constantly worried and distracted, felt depressed, was losing legal cases he felt he should have easily won, and was thinking that he wanted out of the marriage (which—no surprise—was to an intrusive, controlling woman, like his mother).

"I feel like a baseball without any cork at the center," he told me. "I'm just tightly wound string, hollow at the core. And I think people can tell."

"More important," I said, "you can tell."

His eyes filled with tears. "I just don't know what a person does when he has nothing inside him, when he's invented himself the way I have. I don't think you can ever get over that, can you?"

"But you do have something inside you," I said. "You just haven't ever really looked."

What Dennis was missing was his backstory. He had never been willing to go in search of the early painful chapters around which so much of his life still revolved. So he felt empty.

It turned out there was plenty inside Dennis—rage at being controlled by his parents, feelings of weakness resulting from the fact that they had been able to control him, a sense of betrayal that they had done it while professing their love for him, and even feelings of shame that he hadn't done more to stop them.

Once I helped Dennis confront these feelings, he began to feel much less anxious and less depressed, and a lot angrier. He realized that as a young person he had always been afraid to say what he needed or wanted for fear that being his own person would make his parents stop loving him. And that realization helped him summon the determination to free himself from that fear as an adult.

One of the ways Dennis moved toward, then through, and ultimately past the painful chapters of his life story was by deciding to scale back practicing law to three-quarter time so that he could begin studying architecture. That meant confronting many fears, including whether he would be "worth" as much if he didn't make the same amount of money for several years, whether he had only been fooling himself into thinking that he had talent in the area that moved him, and whether his marriage could withstand him investing more in himself and less in his lifestyle.

"She married a guy who made partner in a law firm two years after we tied the knot," Dennis told me. "I start backing off of taking as many cases, that might mean I end up in a solo practice, making half as much. That's not exactly what she bargained for."

"She married *you*," I said. "If that's not really what she bargained for, it might be time to let her know."

"Easier said than done."

It *was*, of course, easier said than done. What I was asking of Dennis was that he confront his fear of being unloved by his parents and unlovable by anyone else. I was asking him to risk being rejected by his wife, which would transport him to his childhood and make him feel very much like a little boy rejected by his parents—alone and exquisitely vulnerable in the world. The difference was that he wasn't little and powerless anymore. It just felt that way.

"Is it easy pretending you're a lawyer?" I asked. "You're already distracted, losing cases you believe you should have easily won."

"It's torture," he said.

"Is it easy pretending your wife loves you when she doesn't really know you?"

He shook his head. "We haven't been together physically for a while. Emotionally . . . probably ever." He thought to himself, then nodded to me. "When it comes right down to it, I guess I have nothing to lose."

"And everything to gain," I said. "Like feeling solid for the first time, even if what you feel is sadness from learning your wife doesn't really love you. Because it would be *your* sadness. It would be *genuine*. And you would find out you can survive it and demand more for yourself."

Dennis took the risk. And he learned something he never could have if he hadn't. He learned that his wife loved him more than he knew. She loved him enough to tell him that his leaving the law scared her but that it didn't scare her nearly as much as the thought of his leaving *her*.

"The only thing is," Dennis told me, "she isn't up for me cutting back to three-quarter time."

I took a deep breath and let it out, starting to feel the disappointment I imagined Dennis must have been feeling. How could anyone expect a person to begin building a new career with less than 25 percent of his time?

"She wants me to cut back to half time," he said. And then he smiled the widest smile he ever had in my office.

I smiled, too. "You were worried she wouldn't love you if you told her who you were," I said. "I think you got your answer."

Dennis had the courage to search for the source of his low self-esteem and to ultimately pursue a craft that spoke to his soul. And that journey had also substantially strengthened his marriage.

Two years later, Dennis left the law entirely to study architecture full-time. He has become a superb and highly sought after architect. That's for two reasons: he loves it, and it's what he was meant to do.

YOUR ULTIMATE REWARD

The cardiologist and philosopher George Sheehan wrote in his book *Running and Being: The Total Experience:*

> Success is not something that can be measured or worn on a watch or hung on the wall. It is not the esteem of colleagues, or the admiration of the community, or the appreciation of patients. Success is the certain knowledge that you have become yourself, the person you were meant to be from all time. That should be reward enough.

The key to writing your own life story and to making the future chapters the best ones of all is being willing to reread the earlier chapters in your story, to face the pain of seeing what you lost in childhood or adolescence or as a young adult. Because that's truly the only way to find yourself again—and begin living the truth.

CHAPTER 12

Protecting Your Children

Living the truth means unearthing the painful chapters of your life story, moving beyond blaming those who have hurt you, and freeing yourself to "write" powerful, loving chapters in the future.

You are truly worthy of the rewards of an examined life—the calm that comes from self-possession, freedom from self-defeating patterns of emotion and behavior, satisfying family and romantic relationships, deeper friendships, more fulfillment from your work, and better health.

But there is an equally important reason to grow by moving through your pain rather than trying to get around it: it's your personal responsibility to do so.

Just as you may have "inherited" the toxic dynamics of your parents or grandparents or even the community in which you were raised, you will pass down to the next generation the pain you fail to face and failed to feel.

I believe that confronting that pain can insulate your children not only from negative patterns of emotion and behavior but from actual mental and physical illnesses.

That wouldn't be true if genetics told the whole story about what gets passed down from parents to their kids. But no study has truly proven that major depression or alcoholism or drug addiction or obesity or compulsive gambling or ADD or being a workaholic is passed from one generation to the next *genetically.* These conditions may "run in" families, but my experience has convinced me that *being raised in those families* is the more significant factor.

If you are an alcoholic, your children's risk of becoming alcoholic is indeed greater than average. But that doesn't prove a rogue gene has hijacked their existence. To believe that genes alone determine your life's path would be to discount how your children are affected by watching you deal with your problems by reaching for a drink, again and again, possibly thousands of times during their developmental years. It's to deny the toll on them of your not being emotionally reliable when they *need* to rely on you for their own emotional development. It's to ignore the fact that watching you search for artificial comfort, rather than finding the courage to deal with the conflicts inherent in *your* marriage, will likely have a negative impact on their future relationships.

I don't believe we will ever find a gene so complex that it dictates, for example, that a woman get in her car, lie to her husband and children about where she is going, drive several miles to the package store, buy a bottle of her favorite vodka, get back in her car, open the bottle, drink the vodka, throw the bottle in a nearby trash can, and use mouthwash to conceal the smell of alcohol on her breath, then drive back home, risking her own life and the lives of others on the road. That would have to be one very complex gene.

True, this woman's nervous system may respond to vodka in a different way from a nonalcoholic's, but that's relevant only once she has made the choice to avoid her underlying emotional pain by drinking.

When people consume large quantities of alcohol despite the fact that it causes them serious problems at work, in their families, and even with the law, their behavior says much more about low self-esteem and how afraid they are of the truth than it does about their genetics or physiology. It says that not feeling their pain is so important to them that they are willing to risk everything rather than face the pain.

It's no different for those whose children watch them overeat or gamble or work ceaselessly to deal with underlying anxiety or sadness or boredom. And it's no different for those whose children see them struggle with low back pain or migraines fueled by stress from unresolved psychological conflicts.

Your children will learn whether to face their pain or to run from it by watching the way you deal with your pain. That's how they "inherit" disorders such as alcoholism and obesity.

How about depression? Can you protect your children from that illness by conquering your own demons? Many psychiatrists would say no. They would point to studies showing that depression is associated with chemical imbalances in the brain, especially with insufficient activity of the neurotransmitter serotonin. Such imbalances, they would argue, are passed from one generation to the next *genetically*. I believe, however, that scientific research will ultimately prove that a child's *environment* determines whether or not any such inherited vulnerability ever turns into a problem.

Here's some evidence to consider. A recent research study (Weissman, M. M., et al. 2006. Remissions in maternal depression and child psychopathology: A STAR*D-child report. *JAMA* 295:1389–1398) demonstrated that the children of mothers with major depression who were treated for that condition and got well were far less likely to become depressed themselves. Obviously, treating the mothers didn't change the *genes* of their children. What changed were the *environments* in which their children were raised. Improving those environments—by making the mothers more available to the children emotionally—improved their chances of staying well.

Would positron-emission tomography (PET) brain scans of the depressed children in the study have shown any abnormalities in serotonin metabolism? Almost certainly. But those abnormalities would not be unexpected in any child living in a very stressful environment.

When I hosted a series of episodes of *The Dr. Keith Ablow Show* called The Anger Illness that focused on mothers who couldn't control their rage and were screaming at and even hitting their sons and daughters, I wasn't surprised to learn that they themselves had been the victims of verbal, emotional, and sometimes sexual abuse as children. For them, anger was a symptom of underlying conditions—including depression, attention deficit disorder, and sleep disorders—fueled by what they had lived through. And I wasn't surprised to see that their children were starting to display the same explosive tempers.

You are an even more powerful force in the lives of your children than you may have imagined—much more powerful than the genes you passed along to them. You can actually inoculate them against psychological suffering and psychiatric illness. The way to do it is to see your life story for what it really is, to own your own pain, and to give them the gift of growing up without having to shoulder it.

THE POWER TO HEAL THE FAMILY

When you try to outdistance your past, you will find it becomes not only your future but that of your children, and perhaps their children as well. The very pain you deny will become your destiny—and theirs.

It is your moral responsibility to do your level best to open the early chapters of your life story and dwell especially on those passages and pages and themes that initially cause you the greatest anxiety. Only by doing so can you overcome the life events and losses which you unconsciously believe have the power to overwhelm you. The truth is that you are strong enough to look deeply at everything you have survived. Doing so will only make you stronger, and living that truth is the greatest gift you can give the people you love.

On my television show, I recently counseled Larry, a man whose three daughters and ex-wife had very little to do with him anymore. He was a large man in his sixties, with powerful hands and a gravelly voice. He had run his home a lot like a jail, with rigid rules and violent punishments. Two of his daughters hadn't been willing to see him for years and had kept their own children away from him. The third had stayed in touch but had kept her distance emotionally.

Why did the daughters ask for my help? They wanted their father to apologize for what he had done to them, which he had never been willing to do. They wanted him to admit that he had made big mistakes as a parent and that those mistakes had hurt them deeply.

There was another reason, of course: with everything they had suffered at his hand, these women still wanted a father. They wanted the man who had known them from birth, who had been present from the very first pages of their life stories, to be part of their lives again and to become part of the lives of his grandchildren—but only if they could believe in their hearts that he had changed.

When a man in his sixties shows up for a meeting—on television—with his three adult daughters, knowing they are intent on detailing the abuse he meted out to them as little girls, it means he has decided to stop running from the past. It means that, at some level, he knows that only the truth can redeem him. So I had real hope Larry would acknowledge that he had caused his daughters to suffer and would say he was sorry.

He didn't start out doing a good job on either score. He denied having threatened his daughters with a stick. He denied having pulled one of his daughters' hair. He denied physically abusing their mother in front of them. He told them it was time to "move on" and put the past behind them.

His daughters ended up in tears, screaming at him. He was traumatizing them all over again, essentially telling them their memories were fabricated and their pain was contrived.

A part of me wondered whether it might be better to suggest to these women that they had the answer they had come to get: their father wasn't willing to tell the truth in order to reestablish relationships with them. It wasn't worth it to him. Out of self-interest, he wanted to drag them into a fictionalized version of their early lives that would deny them their emotional reality and, therefore, their humanity.

That would have been the end of that. It would have been the end of a father's chances to reclaim a connection with his daughters. And it would have been the end of three women's hopes that their father would finally put their needs to be heard and acknowledged as human beings ahead of his own need for control.

The reason the story didn't end that way is that I reminded myself of my core belief—there is no original evil left in the world; everyone is just recycling pain. Using that belief as my guide, I stopped pressing Larry to admit he had abused his daughters and shifted my focus to help him admit that *he* had been abused. I asked him this question: "Who hurt you? Were you hit—or worse—as a child?"

That question elicited genuine emotion from him—a combination of anger and sadness. His jaw churned even as his eyes filled up with tears. He leaned closer to me. "Sure, I got hit," he said. "My father used a stick. His father used barbed wire. Okay?"

At that instant, Larry's daughters began listening in a whole new way. A furrow in one of their brows. A slight tilting of one daughter's head. A tear running down the third's cheek. The ice was beginning to thaw. They were hearing bits of their father's truth—that he had faced violence as a boy from a parent he loved, that he had never learned any other way to interact with his own kids. And when they saw him openly weep about losing his dad when he was just six years old, they were, no doubt, doing the math I was doing in my head: whatever he had endured had been visited upon him before that tender age.

How does a boy get angry at the father who first assaulted him, then died when that boy was just six? How does he ever risk feeling the rage underneath his grief? And if he never digs up that buried treasure, how can he hope to resonate with the pain of daughters to whom that psychological dynamic became contagious?

That's why it had been so hard for so many years for Larry to tell his three daughters that he was sorry for the way he had fathered them: an apology for his behavior was also an indictment of his own father's.

I moved closer to him because I knew that the future of his relationship with his daughters was at stake and that he needed to know it. I looked directly at him. "There are moments that call for remarkable courage in life," I said. "These are moments when you have to see the truth and be willing to speak to it. They can work miracles and change whole lives. But when they're gone, they're gone."

He held my gaze.

"Your father did what he did," I said. "That's an issue for another day. But today, they deserve an apology," I said, nodding at his daughters. "You hurt them." As I spoke the words,

I knew Larry would hear them two ways: *You hurt them. Your father hurt you.* I literally held my breath as he looked at his daughters.

Several seconds passed in silence, then Larry showed the only kind of heroism a man can show in the world. He began living the truth. "I made big mistakes," he told his daughters, with tears starting to come again. "I did things to you that were wrong. Inexcusable. And I'm sorry for them. I never meant to hurt you."

Larry stood up and stepped in front of his three daughters. And one by one, they got up and hugged him.

A man in his sixties had, within an hour, faced pain stored away from age six, pain buried so deep it had dragged his relationship with his daughters down with it. And when he brought it to the surface, far from being destroyed by it, he learned it was a gift powerful enough to bring his daughters back into his life.

THE CYCLE ENDS HERE

Your buried pain is no different from Larry's (or anyone else's). It's the source of your power to change your life and the lives of your children. If, earlier in his life, Larry had been willing to look for his buried pain, he might have spared his daughters a lot of grief. Two of them had had failed marriages, and one had spent years in an abusive relationship. Had Larry been living the truth, he might not have waited until he was more than sixty before starting to build loving relationships not only with his daughters but with his grandchildren as well.

Deep down, you probably know that you exhibit certain behaviors or personality traits that you would not like to see in your children or grandchildren. The work that you've done throughout this book should have helped you bring these to light. Sometimes, however, we need outside verification of how we are actually impacting others.

To that end, I want you to ask five people with whom you are emotionally close and with whom you feel safe—a son or daughter (provided he or she is at least thirteen years old), a dear friend, a brother or sister, a romantic partner, or your spouse—to tell you ways in which your own personality style, choices, or behavior might be negatively influencing them and others around you. Earlier, you may have asked one or all of these people to give you information about your past; you are now seeking information about the present. You should tell them you want honest feedback, no matter how critical, and that you won't be angry with them for giving it to you. And you should do everything you can not to respond with anger, because people who have the courage to tell you the truth are doing so out of love.

For example, you might ask: You've known me long enough to have a handle on what parts of my life need some work. What are they? Be totally honest. I promise I'll never hold anything you say against you.

The parts of my life that, according to my friends and family, need work are:

_____

_____

_____

_____

_____

_____

You might also ask: If you had to suggest that I focus on changing one part of my personality, what would it be? How do you think that change would affect my family?

The one part of my personality that, according to my friends and family, needs to be changed is:

_____

_____

_____

_____

_____

_____

Once you have received this information, write an addendum to your life story. Include the feedback you've gotten from others and how it has affected those around you.

My friends and family tell me that I:
(*Example:* "*My friends and family tell me that I* always brag about how much money I make and the 'designer' purchases I can afford. My children are now beginning to measure their own worth in terms of how much 'stuff' they have.")

_____

_____

_____

_____

_____

_____

This "homework assignment" isn't for the faint of heart. Hearing sincere and hopefully accurate criticism, no matter how well-intentioned, from people you care about takes courage. But it can reward you with invaluable insights into yourself.

Whatever feedback you get, don't stop there. Look for the roots of your unwelcome personality traits, choices, and behaviors in your family of origin. If you are overly concerned with money, maybe you grew up in an atmosphere of poverty and deprivation. If you're perceived by those you love as overly controlling, maybe you grew up with a controlling person, in an environment where you were punished for not being perfect. Or maybe you suffered sudden losses as a child and think that you can avoid unexpected tragedy by micromanaging your life and everyone else's.

State the changes you will make for yourself and your children to end the cycle of your life story.
(*Example:* "My friends and family tell me that I always brag about how much money I make and the 'designer' purchases I can afford. My children are now beginning to measure their own worth in terms of how much 'stuff' they have. *Three changes I will make to improve my situation for myself and my children are:*

1. Keeping in mind that my children are learning from me, I will ask people I trust to make me aware of my bragging habit and will learn to measure my own worth in other ways [such as how I'm improving my relationships with my family and friends].
2. I will stop buying my children every latest gizmo and gadget that comes on the market.
3. I will volunteer to help the less fortunate, and be sure that my children do, too.")

Three changes I will make to improve my situation for myself and my children are:

1. _____

_____

_____

2. _____

_____

_____

3. _____

_____

_____

CHAPTER 13

Living the Truth from
This Day Forward

Our work together began with my promise to deliver you the keys to uncovering your personal truth and facing it, no matter how difficult. I made that promise because I believe to the depths of my soul that lowering your defenses and looking at yourself honestly are the keys to becoming more energized and effective in every facet of your existence. I have seen the results of living the truth in thousands of people with increased self-esteem, improved mood, more successful marriages, more passionate romance, stronger friendships, freedom from addictions, and even relief from physical illnesses. And I have seen the results in my own life.

In turn, I asked you to pledge that you would read *Living the Truth* within thirty days. If you've done so and begun to follow the strategic steps I've outlined, then you are in an ideal position to stop wasting vast quantities of mental energy to keep your past and your pain buried. Now you can start being the genuine and powerful person you were always meant to be. If you haven't begun to act on my practical advice and have arrived at this page without beginning the journey I've urged you to take, then I hope you will make that commitment now.

Moving toward your pain, finding your power, and achieving your true desires won't all be completed when you complete this book. If you continue to face the chapters and themes in your life story that had you on the run, you will continue to be rewarded with new insights about who you are and how you can continue to grow. Honor those insights by returning to reread chapters in this book as you recall the messages they contain. Revisit the exercises within those chapters, adding new truths about what you feel, what you need, and the person you dream about becoming (you can rewrite your answers in your notebook or in the appendix that follows, if you wish). Peel back layer after layer of the denial that has been, for the vast majority of people, building for many, many years.

Living the Truth can be your way of life, not just a lesson on life. Here are a few final suggestions to make that goal a reality.

Find a Trusted Listener

A trusted listener can be your partner as you turn back the pages of your life story and read passages you once avoided. He or she can also give you guidance and encouragement as you write additional pages—whether a new relationship, a new career, a new commitment to sobriety, or a new enthusiasm for revitalizing your marriage. A particularly objective friend may be able to fulfill this role or a sibling might be emotionally aware enough to do it, but a talented therapist is in an ideal position.

Why a therapist? Because a good therapist is like a detective, trainer, and coach rolled into one. He or she will be committed equally to helping you revisit your early injuries and pain (the scene of the crime), recover from them, and move determinedly beyond them to achieve your goals.

How do you know if you've found a good therapist? You'll find yourself saying things like, "I've never thought about my life this way before." "I just feel like I'm seeing things about myself that I haven't been willing to look at." "I don't think I've really started getting to know myself until now." Or you'll find yourself driving home from sessions thinking things like, "Why haven't I ever wanted to know exactly why my mother and my father split up? Couldn't the way they related to each other be affecting my marriage today?" You may suddenly realize the unsupportive person you're living with reminds you an awful lot of your ex-husband and start to wonder why you keep choosing men who undermine you.

If you don't have these kinds of thoughts within six one-hour sessions, try another therapist.

And regardless of who you choose as your listener, make sure you feel challenged, not just comforted by that person. You want someone who will test the truth of your statements by questioning you with a bit of a cynical edge when necessary, someone intent on keeping you honest, someone who'll push you to see things you may still be loath to look at. If talking to the person doesn't feel like work at least some of the time, then save your breath.

Expect Trouble of Another Kind

I've written about the different kinds of trouble you encounter by running from the truth, and I've encouraged you to identify your own. But being a truth teller can come with its own brand of trouble. You may find yourself ostracized, in part or in whole, from friends or family who just can't take your honesty. Maybe your brother would rather forget how tough it was growing up in your childhood home, and you can't quite stay silent about it anymore. Well, good for you, and shame on him. He'll have to look into the darkness eventually, too, in order to see the light. Your job now is to embrace yourself and reality. If people want to drag you back into a life of fiction that deprives you of your humanity (and them of theirs), don't go there. You can't afford to lose yourself again in order to keep the peace or keep their affection.

Focus First on Yourself

While you don't have to stay silent about your new insights, you also don't need to feel compelled to convert your loved ones to a new way of thinking about their lives. As I've said before, no one can outdistance the past. The truth always wins. You can work on yourself and trust that you'll have many opportunities to gently point out that your brother or father or sister or husband or wife or son or daughter is paying a price physically or emotionally for keeping his or her eyes closed to reality.

Your personal growth will be the best way to demonstrate the power of moving toward your pain and confronting it rather than running from it.

Trust the Truth

The beauty of living the truth is that you have a clear path. You needn't run from anything or anyone anymore because you're willing to feel pain—grief over childhood trauma or the loss of treasured relationships, disappointment when others let you down, sadness when a loved one won't support your heartfelt goals. You aren't denying your problems anymore. You're facing them, which gives you the chance to finally solve them.

That doesn't mean you won't have moments of indecision, anxiety, or fear. It's natural to feel those things as you lower your shields and leave comforting fictions behind. But keep your eyes and ears and intuition focused on what is true, and like the North Star, the truth will lead you to personal freedom and fulfillment every time.

Constantly search your heart and mind for what you really feel and think, even when those feelings and thoughts are uncomfortable ones. Speak openly about them, secure in the knowledge that self-revelation is a sign of courage and personal integrity, not weakness. And encourage others to do so by listening with empathy.

Remember, what we have celebrated in our lives does not define or empower us. What we have survived and shared does.

I wish I could watch you use the tools I've given you to grow. I wish I could be there to exchange a knowing glance with you when you look squarely at the truth instead of trying to look away from it. I wish your children and their children could know the example you are setting by opening the early chapters of your life story, reading them, and resolving to write spectacular ones going forward. And I wish you Godspeed.

Afterword

The ideas and exercises I've presented in *Living the Truth* are meant to empower you to embrace reality, especially the painful chapters of your life story that have kept you on the run emotionally. When you give up your fictions, you become genuinely capable of discovering your real talents, finding true love, and connecting much more honestly and powerfully with your friends, family, and children.

Living the Truth is also, however, a key to unlocking realities about the human condition. There are critical extensions of the core principles I've presented here that expand those principles from a strategy for improving your life to a profound way of understanding the people and the world around you. These insights have existed for centuries, always providing a path out of confusion, contempt, and weakness, but we have lost sight of them. I present them here as a lens through which you may see clearly that the human capacity to feel pain is and always has been inextricably tied to the capacity for confidence, courage, and compassion.

Love Everyone, but Trust Those Connected to Truth

While everyone is worthy of your concern and empathy, the principles of *Living the Truth* predict that only those who have recognized the source of their suffering, examined it, and grown from it are *trustworthy*. This is because putting down one's shields, looking in the mirror, and facing the early, complicated chapters of one's life story is the only way to feel pain and grow beyond it.

People who continue to deny their suffering, insisting all is well with them and always has been, can draw you into highly charged, unresolved dramas recycled from their past. And those unresolved dramas can contaminate any story you try to write with them.

For instance, a man may "lovingly" seduce you even while harboring real anger toward women (rooted in unconscious resentment of his controlling or neglectful mother). A business partner may work closely with you on creative ideas even while suspecting you have no loyalty and may therefore withhold critical information from you (because her father was double-crossed by a business partner). A friend may bond with you, then become much too demanding of your time and attention, based on having been rejected by or having lost a sibling in childhood.

How do you recognize those who are trustworthy? Look at how much they rely on shield strategies to get through life. Do they drink excessively, ceaselessly pursue fame or riches, use drugs to get through life, gamble, take inordinate risks, change the topic constantly to avoid addressing anything emotional? Do they romanticize their families of origin, saying they had "perfect parents" or "perfect childhoods" or grew up wealthier than they did? Do they say everything's "great" for them now, that they have the "ideal marriage" or "perfect children" or "wouldn't change a thing"? Remember, people carrying lots of shields can't embrace you. They can't really love you. They're too busy running from the truth.

There's an easy way to identify those in deep denial. Ask anyone who is becoming a significant part of your personal life to tell you his or her life story, especially the parts that were painful. Have the person reflect on the people who were knowingly or unwittingly hurtful. Ask what he or she struggles with emotionally today. Only if the person is willing to tell you about his or her suffering, and only if the story hangs together and feels genuine, are you likely to be with a trustworthy soul.

And always lead by example. Have the courage to talk about your own painful truths early on in personal relationships. If someone is connected with the truth, you'll know it from that person's willingness to listen to yours and his or her palpable desire to hear more of it. If not, be careful to keep your heart safe.

Be Willing to Pay the Price

When you start telling the truth within a family, in a romantic relationship, among friends, or within any community, you may find that others resist it. I have seen dedicated executives fired for questioning the party line in companies that are headed for financial disaster. I have seen family members become angry at, poke fun at, and ostracize the "truth teller." I have seen mothers and fathers cease all communication with their children when those children stop settling for disabling family fictions and finally face the real, painful, and ultimately freeing facts of their life stories. I have seen husbands file for divorce rather than embrace the opportunity to enrich their marriages when their wives insist on honest communication (and vice versa).

However, I have also seen businesses turned around after heeding the warnings of one whistle-blower. I have seen friendships deepen dramatically. I have seen many family members begin to relate to one another in stronger, more genuine ways. I have seen marriages revitalized.

Keep this at the front of your mind: whether you are embraced or isolated for living the truth, the price is always lower than the cost of running from that truth. Shared fictions—within families or among friends—are false, temporary comforts. The emotional toll of avoiding reality only gets steeper over time. And the last thing you can afford to lose is your authenticity, your*self*.

Bring Along Those You Can

Living the truth will attract those who welcome honesty and will provoke or frighten those who fear it. But sometimes those who are fearful can be inspired to overcome their resistance and put down their own shields when your communication with them is open, understanding, and forgiving. If you were to make it clear to your spouse, for example, that you cannot tolerate his drinking any longer (which, perhaps, you tolerated because you were powerless to oppose your father's drinking), you can simultaneously invite him to live the truth with you. "There's got to be a *reason* you're drinking," you might say, "and if you're willing to really dig deep to discover it, I am willing to go on that journey with you. But it would mean showing me good evidence you're ready to get sober—like going to detox." Or if you were taken advantage of by a dear friend, you might extend her a hand and say, "There has to be a *reason* you would violate our trust. Maybe your trust was violated at some point in your life. If you tell me, I'll still be hurt, but it could help me understand and help us get past this—together."

Some people will take your hand and be inspired by your love for yourself, for them, and for the truth. Others will not. Making the offer is always worthwhile.

The Truth Takes Its Own Time

Just as unresolved childhood pain has its own gravitational pull, drawing us back into destructive orbits, truth has its own energy. And nothing is more powerful than truth.

Not everyone will have an immediate positive response when you drop your shields, look in the mirror, and begin living the truth. Once they see how your more honest way of looking at yourself, at them, and at the world is working to your benefit, however, they will likely come around. Or they may ask for your guidance when their own avoidance of the truth has caused them more suffering.

The truth always wins in good time—even if that time is later than you would have hoped. Keeping that in mind will help you to be compassionate and accepting when others come to their own truths.

Looking for Leadership? Look to Those Who Have Suffered (and Say So)

In recent decades, our notion of strength in this culture has come to be synonymous with the denial of pain and doubt. The lives of our leaders have to be storybook tales of success and unwavering strength. But the truth is that those who have known adversity and have faced the suffering inherent in it know the most about humanity. They are the ones who can resonate most deeply with the suffering of others. They know the real stakes of any conflict, the toll of any prejudice, or the tragic scope of any natural disaster because they can truly *feel* for those involved.

Abraham Lincoln and Winston Churchill, arguably two of the greatest leaders of all time, both suffered from depression. Both had troubled childhoods. And if they were beginning their political careers today and their psychological struggles were known, they would probably be unelectable.

Emotionally open and therefore honest men and women, carrying fewer shields, are the only ones who can effectively formulate and execute honest agendas to heal our wounds and advance our good and humane ideas. For true and bold vision, look to those who have the courage to say they have known disappointment and fear and grief, yet have kept their hearts and minds open, and continue to dream great dreams.

Know That Opposition to Truth Can Be Organized, Even Violent

Just as individuals deploy shield strategies to avoid seeing painful realities, so too can groups of people, even whole nations.

The first response to truth tellers who challenge the status quo is often quarantine—whether by mocking their views, silencing them through censorship, or imprisoning them. And when a culture is desperate to deny painful realities (such as past weaknesses, current inequities, or future threats), it can act violently to remove the individuals who most clearly see those realities.

This is a way to understand the killings of Christ, Abraham Lincoln, Reverend Martin Luther King Jr., and Gandhi. It explains the long imprisonment of Nelson Mandela. It also means that the ideas with the greatest potential to transform society may well reside with those initially marginalized by that society.

When we are most inclined *not* to listen, we should be careful to listen most closely.

A Promise, a Pledge, a Prayer

I started this book with a promise that I would do my best to help you find out what's been limiting you and to give you powerful tools to overcome it. In turn, I asked you to pledge that you would faithfully try to overcome the resistance to this book that was likely to arise within you, to read it within thirty days, and to begin courageously uncovering your personal truth.

I hope you believe I have delivered what I promised, and that you have made good on your pledge.

This journey, of course, is much longer than thirty days. It is the journey of a lifetime. So as I leave you to it, it is with this prayer:

May you always know
you need not run from any chapter of your life story,
that you are as strong as anything you are willing to feel,
that facing pain is a source of power,
and that love for yourself and for others is invincible.

The Pain-to-Power
Prescription

The exercises in this book are meant to help you unravel the mystery of your life story. I present them here for you again, one after another, so that you can use them as you wish, perhaps photocopying them and repeating them more than once yourself or giving the pages to a loved one to prompt his or her own journey of self-discovery.

By completing the exercises a second and third time, even if it means repeating much of what you've written before, you will focus the insights you've already gained.

CHAPTER 1:
THE PAIN-TO-POWER PRINCIPLE

I chose to read Living the Truth *because:*
(*Example:* "*I chose to read* Living the Truth *because* I need to change my stressful marriage.")

1. _____

2. _____

3. _____

Now rewrite your sentences, being as specific as possible about the problems.

I chose to read Living the Truth *because:*
(*Example:* "*I chose to read* Living the Truth *because* I need to stop drinking, which I do to calm my anxiety about taking care of my family.")

1. _____

_____

2. _____

_____

3. _____

_____

CHAPTER 2:
LIVING BEHIND SHIELDS

My shield strategy is:
(*Example:* "*My shield strategy is* staying on the computer for hours at a time.")

1. _____

2. _____

3. _____

4. _____

5. _____

6. _____

My antishield strategy is:
(*Example:* "*My antishield strategy is* limiting my time on the computer to one hour in the evening, after dinner.")

1. _____

2. _____

3. _____

4. _____

5. _____

6. _____

In order to anticipate, identify, and overcome the use of shield strategies (whether old or new), it helps to keep track of them. I advise you to make several copies of this page in order to chart your progress each week.

Week _____ (one, two, etc.)

My shield strategies:
(e.g., overeating, smoking, etc.)

Intensity level
(1–10,
1 being least)

_____   _____

_____   _____

_____   _____

My antishield strategies:
(e.g., visit a nutritionist and follow a new diet)

Success
(1–10,
1 being least)

_____   _____

_____   _____

_____   _____

Emerging (newly deployed) shield strategies:
(e.g., constantly playing video games)

Intensity level
(1–10,
1 being least)

_____   _____

_____   _____

_____   _____

	Success
New antishield strategies:	(1–10,
(e.g., limit video game use to one hour per day)	1 being least)

_____   _____

_____   _____

_____   _____

CHAPTER 3:
UNDERSTANDING THE FOUR FICTIONS

What's your favorite story about your childhood—the one you most like to tell when people ask about your early years?

_____

_____

_____

_____

What's your least favorite story about your childhood—the one that includes the last thing you'd want a friend, a lover, or your spouse to know?

_____

_____

_____

_____

What part of your life story as a child or young adult took the most strength to survive?

_____

_____

_____

_____

What are the qualities you struggle most to make sure people know about you? (Your intelligence? Your physical strength? How many friends you have?)

_____

_____

_____

Why are these qualities so important to you? Complete the sentence below:
(*Examples:* "*I want people to know how* smart *I am because* my father always thought I was pretty but 'not too bright.' " "*I want people to know how* well-liked *I am because* I was so unpopular in high school.")
I want people to know how _____ *I am because:*

_____

_____

_____

I want people to know how _____ *I am because:*

_____

_____

_____

I want people to know how _____ *I am because:*

_____

_____

_____

The people I could most rely on as a child or young adult were:

_____

_____

_____

The people I wish had been more reliable when I was a child or young adult were:

_____

_____

_____

The individuals from the previous statement let me down by:

_____

_____

_____

ere any economic, social, or cultural circumstances of your youth that were painful to you? List them here.

_____

_____

_____

What have you done to cover up or compensate for those circumstances (e.g., living to make money because you grew up poor or denying your own roots because they made you feel different from others around you)?

_____

_____

_____

_____

_____

_____

CHAPTER 4:
THE FOUR FACES OF PAIN

Which face of pain do you wear (e.g., interpersonal conflicts, physical illnesses, pathological behaviors, psychiatric disturbances)?

My face(s) of pain is/are:
(*Examples: "My face of pain is* unexplained physical illness. I get headaches almost every day, and my doctor cannot find a cause."

"*My face of pain is* interpersonal conflict. I'm always hooking up with controlling men who don't care about my needs.")

1. _____

_____

_____

2. _____

_____

_____

3. _____

_____

_____

4. _____

_____

_____

CHAPTER 5:
WHY WE DENY THE TRUTH

Think about the people who were most important to you during your childhood years, and answer the questions below.

In my story, as a child and as a young adult, who was there for me with unconditional love?

_____

_____

In my story, as a child and as a young adult, who did I feel put conditions on their love, and what were those conditions?
(*Examples:* "My father *loved me when I* excelled at sports." "My sister *loved me when I* took the blame for her misdeeds.")
My _____ *loved me when I:*

_____

_____

_____

And that made me feel:
(*Example:* "My sister *loved me when I took the blame for her misdeeds, and that made me feel* that everything that went wrong was somehow my fault.")

_____

_____

_____

The events or patterns of behavior displayed by my mother or father that were not *loving included:*
(*Example:* "*The events or patterns of behavior displayed by my mother or father that were* not *loving included* when my mother constantly asked me to take her side in arguments she had with my father. Or when my father told me I could be beautiful *if* I lost weight.")

_____

_____

_____

_____

_____

_____

If I were to write to my mother or father or a sibling (or someone else who was really important to me) about the way(s) in which his or her love was really hard to feel deep down, I would say: (*Example:* "Dad, you're always saying how much you love me and how special I was to you growing up. But it's pretty hard to really *feel* that, considering the fact that you only visited every other weekend after you divorced mom. Mom says you had 'full visitation' and could have been around a lot more. Why weren't you? I think I've always sort of assumed that I was an embarrassment to you or an inconvenience.")

_____

_____

_____

_____

_____

_____

_____

_____

In my story, as a child and as a young adult, the person who made me feel safest was:
(*Example:* "*In my story, as a child and as a young adult, the person who made me feel safest was* my older brother.")

_____

But being close to that person exposed me to some pain, too, including:
(*Example:* "*But being close to that person exposed me to some pain, too, including* the fact that my older brother was ten years older than me, and I felt abandoned when he went away to college and left me at home with my verbally abusive father.")

_____

_____

_____

_____

And that made me feel:
(*Example:* "*My brother abandoned me when he went away to college, and that made me feel* that men will let you down when you need them most.")

_____

_____

_____

_____

If _____ *had not been in my life as a child, I would have felt totally alone. But dealing with him/her certainly meant coping with:*
(*Example:* "*If* Uncle Fred *had not been in my life as a child, I would have felt totally alone. But dealing with him certainly meant coping with* the fact that he was a terrible alcoholic.")

_____

_____

_____

_____

The reason I always wince when my mother/father/sister/brother/ childhood friend talks about how great things were for us growing up is:
(*Example:* "*The reason I always wince when my mother/father/ sister/brother/childhood friend talks about how great things were for us growing up is* that it wasn't so great because we were so poor.")

_____

_____

_____

_____

The most anxiety-provoking part of my childhood was:
(*Example:* "*The most anxiety-provoking part of my childhood was* when my brother was diagnosed with leukemia, and my parents got very, very quiet about the whole thing. It made me sort of feel like I might get sick, too, and I remember constantly look-

ing in the mirror to see if I was getting pale. But I also felt guilty for worrying about myself so much when my brother was the one with the illness.")

Even though I had a pretty decent life growing up, I'd like to spare my own kids:
(*Example: "Even though I had a pretty decent life growing up, I'd like to spare my own kids* the constant moving around we did. I think it made it tough for me to form friendships back then. But I also think it makes me feel as if all friendships are temporary, even now. I sometimes think I end friendships over little arguments just because I'm always thinking they're about to end anyway.")

CHAPTER 6:
WHY WE REPEAT THE PAST

What painful part of your childhood are you reproducing today (e.g., are you putting up with emotional abuse from your spouse because you got used to being criticized relentlessly by a parent you desperately needed as a child)?

_____

_____

_____

_____

What painful dynamic are you running from by trying to avoid anything that reminds you of it (e.g., are you so wary of any criticism that reminds you of your hypercritical parents that you turn your back on anyone who questions you in any way)?

_____

_____

_____

_____

I wish I had had more control over my life as a child or adolescent when:
(*Example:* "*I wish I had had more control over my life as a child or adolescent when* my parents took me out of public school and registered me for parochial school. I wasn't doing well in classes because my creativity was being stifled, and it only got worse in an even more structured environment.")

_____

_____

_____

_____

If I could have edited out one event from my early life experiences, it would have been:
(*Example:* "*If I could have edited out one event from my early life experiences, it would have been* the day my parents adopted a third child. It isn't that I don't love him, but he needed a great deal of their attention, and I have to admit I felt pushed aside.")

_____

_____

_____

_____

In the space below, write down the patterns you see throughout your life. Think about both your personal and your professional life, and what situations you seem to find yourself in again and again.

Make a list of the patterns that have consistently shown up in your personal life:

_____

_____

_____

_____

_____

_____

Make a list of the patterns that have consistently shown up in your professional life:

_____

_____

_____

_____

_____

What events early in my life may have set my patterns in motion?

_____

_____

_____

_____

_____

_____

_____

Write a compelling life story that explains why you find your-self facing the specific problems you listed in the previous chapters. For example, broken marriages often have their roots in strained early relationships with parents—or between parents. Depression fueling alcohol abuse often has its roots in feelings of being unloved, unwanted, or powerless. Being abused physically or emotionally today often means that one got used to being physically or emotionally abused long ago. There is no right or wrong way to write this story—just be certain that it links your current problem(s) with what you experienced much earlier in your life.

_____

_____

_____

_____

_____

_____

_____

_____

_____

_____

_____

_____

_____

_____

_____

_____

CHAPTER 7:
ARE WE HARDWIRED TO RUN FROM PAIN?

If people knew everything about me, the thing that might end up costing me their friendship or affection or respect would be:

_____

_____

_____

_____

_____

The reason I think that revelation would be so troubling to people is:

_____

_____

_____

_____

_____

But if I were going to try to tell any person everything about me, I would tell:

_____

I would choose that person because:

_____

_____

_____

_____

_____

CHAPTER 8:
UNDERSTANDING THE FAMILY FICTION

Do you suspect your family has a fiction? What do you think it is? (*Example:* "I've always been told that my sister left home for a year to live with my aunt in Arizona because she needed the dry air. I believe there is more to this story that I have not been told.")

_____

_____

_____

_____

_____

Because our life stories often veer into fiction while we are still children, finding our truth can be greatly accelerated by reaching out to others for facts that have been kept from us or which we have forgotten. Ask friends and family what they may know about your childhood and adolescent years. After you speak to your "sources," write down what they've told you, because you might want to be able to reflect upon what was said, and it will be helpful to have a written record to help you remember.

_____

_____

_____

_____

_____

_____

_____

_____

Write your life story again (or add to the one you've already written on page 282), incorporating the information you've learned from others about yourself, your childhood, your family, and your family fiction.

_____

_____

_____

_____

_____

_____

_____

_____

_____

_____

_____

_____

_____

CHAPTER 9:
FACING THE TRUTH IS NOT ABOUT BLAME

Sometimes it's easier to see how the past influences the present and determines the future when you see those forces operating in someone else's life. Write a story about how your parents' personalities and behavior patterns have been shaped by the experiences each lived through growing up.

Stories you've learned about your mother:

_____

_____

_____

_____

_____

_____

_____

Stories you've learned about your father:

_____

_____

_____

_____

_____

_____

_____

Think about what unresolved issues in your parents' life stories may have been unwittingly handed down to you. Ask yourself how your history of struggling to become genuine and powerful really goes back generations.

Have my mother's issues been handed down to me? If so, how?

_____

_____

_____

_____

_____

_____

_____

Have my father's issues been handed down to me? If so, how?

_____

_____

_____

_____

_____

_____

_____

The toughest challenges my mother faced in becoming a complete and loving person were:
(*Example: "The toughest challenges my mother faced in becoming a complete and loving person were* her learning disability and resulting low grades, which made everyone around her think she was unintelligent for so many years. That set her up to be valued only for her looks, and she never developed real self-esteem.")

_____

_____

_____

_____

The toughest challenges my father faced in becoming a complete and loving person were:

(*Example:* "*The toughest challenges my father faced in becoming a complete and loving person were* his own mother's neglect and the way she set him up to need so much attention and reassurance from the women in his life.")

_____

_____

_____

_____

_____

If I could have magically spared my parents pain from their past, I would have rewritten their life histories without the following events:

(*Example:* "*If I could have magically spared my parents pain from their past, I would have rewritten their life histories without the following events:* the loss of my paternal grandfather to heart disease when my father was eleven, and the senseless argument that ended my mother's relationship with her sister. I don't think my dad ever felt secure again, and expressed that by trying to control everything and everyone around him. And I think my mother put up with it to avoid the kind of blowup she'd had with my aunt.")

_____

_____

_____

_____

_____

_____

While my mother was far from perfect, she improved on the kind of parenting she experienced as a girl in this way:
(*Example: "While my mother was far from perfect, she improved on the kind of parenting she experienced as a girl in this way:* she still had a bad habit of yelling like everyone in her family, but unlike her own mother, she never hit me.")

_____

_____

_____

_____

While my father was far from perfect, he improved on the kind of parenting he experienced as a boy in this way:
(*Example: "While my father was far from perfect, he improved on the kind of parenting he experienced as a boy in this way:* my father's own parents didn't go to college, and neither did he. And even though he was relentlessly critical of my decision to pursue a career in music, he did work his heart out to make sure I could go to college, even when I switched my concentration from engineering to music studies.")

_____

_____

_____

_____

CHAPTER 10:
GETTING TO YOUR TRUE DESIRE

Getting to your true desire is a three-step process: identify the trouble spots that need the most attention; embrace the truth behind your trouble spots; and devise a plan to turn your personal truth into your personal treasure. Now you're going to zero in on the specific areas that hold the most promise for dramatic change. Filling in the exercises below will help you make that process easier.

List three things about which you are ambivalent:

1. _____

2. _____

3. _____

I'm most *ambivalent about:*

_____

List three things you are secretive about:

1. _____

2. _____

3. _____

I'm most *secretive about:*

_____

List three things you are embarrassed by or about:

1. _____

2. _____

3. _____

I'm most *embarrassed by or about:*

_____

List three of your greatest fears:

1. _____

2. _____

3. _____

My greatest *fear is:*

_____

Three behaviors or personality traits that bother me when I ob-serve them in others are:

1. _____

2. _____

3. _____

The behavior or personality trait that bothers me the most *is:*

_____

My three worst relationships since leaving my childhood home have been:

1. _____

2. _____

3. _____

My absolute worst relationship was:

_____

The three worst conflicts I've encountered on the job have been:

1. _____

2. _____

3. _____

The worst conflict I've encountered on the job has been:

_____

I feel like giving up completely when:

1. _____

2. _____

3. _____

The situation that most makes me want to give up is:

_____

The three times I remember going way overboard defending myself were:

1. _____

2. _____

3. _____

The one time I went the farthest *overboard was:*

_____

I call the list of *most, worst,* etc., responses above your "Life Story Clues," because once you realize what they are, they can help you solve the mystery of why you behave the way you do. Below, list the nine Life Story Clues you filled in previously (e.g., I'm *most* ambivalent about . . . ; I'm *most* secretive about . . .).

My Life Story Clues:
1. *I'm* most *ambivalent about:*

_____

_____

_____

2. *I'm* most *secretive about:*

_____

_____

_____

3. *I'm* most *embarrassed by or about:*

_____

_____

_____

4. *My* greatest *fear is:*

_____

_____

_____

5. *The behavior or personality trait that bothers me the* most *is:*

_____

_____

_____

6. *My absolute* worst *relationship was:*

_____

_____

_____

7. *The* worst *conflict I've encountered on the job has been:*

_____

_____

_____

8. *The situation that* most *makes me want to give up is:*

_____

_____

_____

9. *The one time I went the* farthest *overboard was:*

_____

_____

_____

In the section below, transcribe each of the Life Story Clues from above and write the word "because" beside it. Then answer the "why" question by creating a sensible and persuasive sentence that ties today's troubles to yesterday's truths. Here's an example: "*My absolute* worst *relationship was* with a man who criticized me all the time about my weight *because* my father used to do the same thing. That made me wonder how anyone could do that to someone he loved."

Each sentence you've completed is a very clear sign of what matters to you in life. Each contains a trouble spot and its roots in the past. And each, therefore, points in a direction you need to grow for you to find peace, pleasure, and fulfillment. Here's how to start right now. Below, complete this half sentence:

Therefore, if I'm really going to show courage and use my pain to become more powerful and move in the direction of my true desires, I'm going to take the chance to:
Here's an example: "*My absolute* worst *relationship was* with a man who criticized me all the time about my weight *be-*

cause my father used to do the same thing. That made me wonder how anyone could do that to someone he loved. *Therefore, if I'm really going to show courage and use my pain to become more powerful and move in the direction of my true desires, I'm going to take the chance to* stop avoiding situations in which I might be criticized. And when a friend or romantic partner is critical of me, I'm going to ask him or her to explain more about his or her feelings, instead of running away from the situation."

Complete your Life Story Clues here:

1. *I'm* most *ambivalent about:*

_____

_____

_____

Therefore, if I'm really going to show courage and use my pain to become more powerful and move in the direction of my true desires, I'm going to take the chance to:

_____

_____

_____

2. *I'm* most *secretive about:*

_____

_____

_____

Therefore, if I'm really going to show courage and use my pain to become more powerful and move in the direction of my true desires, I'm going to take the chance to:

_____

_____

_____

3. *I'm* most *embarrassed by or about:*

_____

_____

_____

Therefore, if I'm really going to show courage and use my pain to become more powerful and move in the direction of my true desires, I'm going to take the chance to:

_____

_____

_____

4. My greatest *fear is:*

_____

_____

_____

Therefore, if I'm really going to show courage and use my pain to become more powerful and move in the direction of my true desires, I'm going to take the chance to:

_____

_____

_____

5. *The behavior or personality trait that bothers me the* most *is:*

_____

_____

_____

Therefore, if I'm really going to show courage and use my pain to become more powerful and move in the direction of my true desires, I'm going to take the chance to:

_____

_____

_____

6. *My absolute* worst *relationship was:*

_____

_____

_____

Therefore, if I'm really going to show courage and use my pain to become more powerful and move in the direction of my true desires, I'm going to take the chance to:

_____

_____

_____

7. *The* worst *conflict I've encountered on the job has been:*

_____

_____

_____

Therefore, if I'm really going to show courage and use my pain to become more powerful and move in the direction of my true desires, I'm going to take the chance to:

_____

_____

_____

8. *The situation that* most *makes me want to give up is:*

_____

_____

_____

Therefore, if I'm really going to show courage and use my pain to become more powerful and move in the direction of my true desires, I'm going to take the chance to:

_____

_____

_____

9. *The one time I went the farthest overboard was:*

_____

_____

_____

Therefore, if I'm really going to show courage and use my pain to become more powerful and move in the direction of my true desires, I'm going to take the chance to:

_____

_____

_____

CHAPTER 11:
ENVISIONING THE FUTURE

Write down your hopes for yourself as though you were writing to a dear friend in your circumstances. Start with "I hope that you . . ."

_____

_____

_____

_____

_____

_____

_____

Write down three specific steps you can take right now to demonstrate you are growing beyond the toxic lessons you learned as a child (e.g., you can call a therapist for an appointment, connect with your sister whom you haven't seen in years, enroll in a class or workshop, etc.).

1. _____

_____

2. _____

_____

3. _____

_____

Consider each of the steps above. Expand each one into a story about what you would be like if you were to take this step — how your life might change.

(*Example:* "I realize that I never trusted my sister, because my mother always pitted us against each other. If I apologize to her, I can have much richer friendships with women and stop relying on men to fulfill all my needs. Then maybe I can have a balanced relationship and actually find one man who wants to have an equal partnership. That might even lead to marriage and children.")

My step 1 story:

_____

_____

_____

_____

_____

_____

My step 2 story:

_____

_____

_____

_____

_____

_____

My step 3 story:

_____

_____

_____

_____

_____

_____

_____

CHAPTER 12:
PROTECTING YOUR CHILDREN

Ask five people with whom you are emotionally close and with whom you feel safe to tell you ways in which your own personality style, choices, or behavior might be negatively influencing them and others around you. Earlier, you may have asked one or all of these people to give you information about your past; you are now seeking information about the present. For example, you might ask: You've known me long enough to have a handle on what parts of my life need some work. What are they? Be totally honest. I promise I'll never hold anything you say against you.

The parts of my life that, according to my friends and family, need work are:

_____

_____

_____

_____

_____

You might also ask: If you had to suggest that I focus on changing one part of my personality, what would it be? How do you think that change would affect my family?

The one part of my personality that, according to my friends and family, needs to be changed is:

_____

_____

_____

_____

_____

_____

Once you have received this information, write an addendum to the life story from pages 282 and 285. Include the feedback you've gotten from others and how it has affected those around you.

My friends and family tell me that I:
(*Example:* "My friends and family tell me that I always brag about how much money I make and the 'designer' purchases I can afford. My children are now beginning to measure their own worth in terms of how much 'stuff' they have.")

_____

_____

_____

_____

_____

_____

_____

Three changes I will make to improve my situation for myself and my children are:

1. _____

   _____

   _____

2. _____

   _____

   _____

3. _____

   _____

   _____

Acknowledgments

Living the Truth would not be in your hands were it not for the skill and dedication of my agent, Richard Pine of InkWell Management, and my editor, Tracy Behar of Little, Brown and Company.

I am deeply indebted to Michael Pietsch and Sophie Cottrell, publisher and associate publisher of Little, Brown and Company. My invaluable team there also includes Heather Rizzo, Marlena Bittner, Karen Landry, and Brooke Stetson.

Sharyn Kolberg, Marilyn Firth, Suzanne Turcotte, Lisa Hackner, Chris Burch, Julian Geiger, Molly Zier, and Dr. Rock Positano provided critical insights and support.

Cathy Chermol, Executive Producer of *The Dr. Keith Ablow Show*, has amazed me with her dedication to the ideas presented in this book, but also with her loyalty, work ethic, and creativity.

Finally, I thank my parents, Jeanette and Allan, my sister, Karen, my wife, Debbie, and my children, Devin and Cole, for their love and understanding through all the long nights of writing and all the years we have shared together.